LIBRARIANS, HISTORIANS, AND NEW OPPORTUNITIES FOR DISCOURSE

LIBRARIANS, HISTORIANS, AND NEW OPPORTUNITIES FOR DISCOURSE

A Guide for Clio's Helpers

JOEL D. KITCHENS

AN IMPRINT OF ABC-CLIO, LLC

Santa Barbara, California • Denver, Colorado • Oxford, England

Library of Congress Cataloging-in-Publication Data

Kitchens, Joel D.
  Librarians, historians, and new opportunities for discourse : a guide
for Clio's helpers / Joel D. Kitchens.
     pages cm
  Includes bibliographical references and index.
  ISBN 978-1-59884-625-6 (pbk.) — ISBN 978-1-59884-626-3 (ebook)
1. Historical libraries.   2. Libraries—Special collections—History.
3. History—Bibliography—Methodology.   4. Library orientation for history
students.   5. Historiography.   6. History—Research.   7. History—
Methodology.   I. Title.
  Z675.H5K58 2012
    026.9—dc23   2012008482

ISBN: 978-1-59884-625-6
EISBN: 978-1-59884-626-3

16   15   14   13   12   1   2   3   4   5

This book is also available on the World Wide Web as an eBook.
Visit www.abc-clio.com for details.

Libraries Unlimited
An Imprint of ABC-CLIO, LLC

ABC-CLIO, LLC
130 Cremona Drive, P.O. Box 1911
Santa Barbara, California 93116-1911

This book is printed on acid-free paper ∞

Manufactured in the United States of America

CONTENTS

Introduction   *xi*

1 Overview of History   1

Brief History of History   1

Major Fields within History   2

Major Research Methods Used   4

Use and Characteristics of Primary and Secondary Sources   5

Scholarly Production: Books, Book Reviews, More Books, Scholarly
 Articles, and More Books!   6

Emerging Areas   7

Overlap with Other Areas in the Library   8

Conclusion   10

2 Learning Your New Landscape   11

Materials Needed   11

What Is and May Not Be Available (the Truth Is *Not* Always Out There)   13

Major Historians and Their Evolving Methodologies   15

Continuing Education   17

Mentorship   17

Library Association Divisions   18

Major Historical Societies and Organizations   19

Electronic Discussion Groups   20

Conferences   20

Conclusion   22

3 Getting to Know and Understand Your Local Audience   23

Talking to the Academic Department   23

Meeting Faculty on Their Own Turf   24

What Are the Local Institution's Needs?   28

Conclusion   34

4 Reference Services and Access to Material 35

Get to Know Your Collection 35

The Reference Interview 36

Catalogs and Cataloging 42

The Reference Collection 43

Major Indexes: Accessing Secondary Materials Electronically 44

Other Types of Information 45

Archival Materials 46

Printed Guides, Bibliographies, Encyclopedias, Landmark Works 47

Reference on Location 50

24/7 Reference (or Close to It) 51

Conclusion 52

5 Information Literacy for Historians 55

The History Curriculum 56

History Components in Other Disciplines 60

Building Instructional Presentations 62

Collaborative Partnering on Assignments 64

Intervention with the Instructor 65

Too Much of a Good Thing? 67

Conclusion 68

6 Defining the History Collection 69

Challenges of History to Collection Development Policies 69

Defining *Scholarly* and *Historical* 71

Textbook Considerations 74

Serials 74

Evaluating Electronic Full Text 78

Media and Web-Based Materials 79

Microforms 81

Newspapers 83

Conclusion 85

7 Selection and Acquisitions Tools 87

Budget Considerations 87

Building a Foundation 93

Using Approval Plans 95

Review Sources 97

Getting Prize Books 98

Assessing the Collection 100

Promoting the Collections 101

Open Stacks or Special Collections 101

Conclusion 102

8 Maturing as a History Librarian 105

Progressive Journey 105

Setbacks 107

Navigating Departmental Politics 108

Indicators of Progress   109
Sharing Knowledge as a Senior Subject Librarian   110
Conclusion   110

Reference List and Recommended Readings   *113*

Index   *119*

INTRODUCTION

You stare at the two e-mails in disbelief. The first announces your colleague who is the subject specialist librarian for history at your library is leaving soon for greener pastures elsewhere. The second e-mail from the library administration announces that you will be named to take over the history specialist's liaison duties in collection development, reference, and bibliographic instruction for the foreseeable future because a hiring freeze has just been implemented.

But maybe you hated history in college, or feel it has been too many years since you last took a history class. Then you remember the basic history classes you took as an undergraduate. History is just the names of a bunch of dead kings, presidents, and dates of obscure battles, right? Anyone would know what a history book is, right? Besides, call number systems make it easy. Aren't all of the books for history classified LC Call Numbers (LCCN) C, D, E, and F, or the Dewey 900s?

Well, no; not exactly.

History is actually an exceptionally complex discipline that makes extensive use of a wide variety of library sources in myriad formats requiring an extremely diligent and open-minded approach. Historians and their students are some of the heaviest users of a library's resources and helping them find what they need for research and class assignments is a challenge. Building, maintaining, and assisting with access and reference for a high-quality collection of materials useful to historians need not be difficult, but librarians new to this role must be aware of some important issues. Because the discipline of history has changed over the past fifty years, more books of interest to historians are now found in every call number range. The discipline has become more inclusive of underrepresented groups and societal issues and expanded to include methodologies from other fields. History at the collegiate level often bears little resemblance to the simple stories from grade school about George Washington and the cherry tree or John Wayne's Wild West. The current generation of historians wrestles with knotty problems of group (e.g., ethnic, gender, racial, socioeconomic, etc.) identity at various points in the past; they debate issues of power, resistance, assimilation, agency, and the changing dynamics between the colonizers and the colonized; they examine issues of changing economic times and the effects on populations using less efficient methods; they look for the effects of technologies that broke new ground and opened new ways of doing things for our ancestors and how these new ways affected their descendants. As a result of these sweeping changes, the single most important issue is that history materials can be found throughout call number ranges, not just Library of Congress Call Numbers (LCCN) C-F, or the Dewey 900s. As such, call number systems alone are inadequate measures to define history books for reference activities, collection development policy statements, approval plans, collection use studies, or any other statistical report. Another important issue librarians must remember is that historians prize materials created in the time period they are researching (primary sources). These materials left by earlier generations are the building blocks of historical research and professional, research historians must make extensive use of them. These materials may be available in many different formats—as a rare, physical special collection item, as a microform reproduction, or a digitally scanned image—each with its own set of challenges and advantages.

In order to get the newest generation of historical researchers accustomed to using these materials, instructors often require their students to find and use these primary sources in term papers even at nonresearch institutions and community college environments. This leads to another issue any librarian must face, that of knowing who will actually be using the collection and in what manner. Academic librarians should not hesitate to walk over to the history department and talk with faculty about their research topics and information needs; the results can be surprising. Librarians working at Association of Research Libraries (ARL) institutions will have some different goals, priorities, level of resource needs, and missions than those working at local community colleges. Each type of institution presents its own set of challenges and responsibilities, and librarians must be mindful of these as they work to build and guide access to a collection that meets both the short-term needs and long-term goals of their particular institution. Librarians at public academic institutions may additionally need to keep in touch with local schools and genealogical groups to better ascertain their needs as well, since they are answerable to the taxpayers at some level. With this information, the history librarian can better serve the reference, research, and teaching needs for all groups within the local user population.

This book is designed to be a practical guide to help librarians at any experience level in North American academic libraries whose background is not history quickly become familiar with many of the issues, tools, and concerns for building and maintaining quality collections, providing effective reference service and library instruction, and developing successful liaison relationships with professional historians and their students, as well as other researchers with history-related interests in the user community. Sadly, academia has not been immune to the economic crisis that has rocked the first decade of the twenty-first century. As many libraries reduce professional positions, it very well may be that librarians with limited knowledge of a particular subject find themselves placed in a role where there was once expertise. You, the reader, may be an assistant department head in technical services with two decades of experience, but now find yourself thrust into the public services side as liaison because of budget reductions. The author hopes this book will help ease the steep learning curve, at least for the discipline of history, or as one encounters historical research in the context of other disciplines.

A secondary purpose of this book is to encourage dialogue between librarians and historians by giving each some idea of the needs and challenges the other is facing. Libraries are facing many challenges on a variety of fronts. Budgets have been savaged by the economic downturn in this opening decade of the twenty-first century, and many libraries have been forced to choose between reducing collections budgets or saving staffing levels, while some libraries may only wish they had been given that choice. The digital revolution and ever-increasing electronic resources have brought great promises for libraries and how they serve their communities, but not without some peril. Digital resources may not always be the least expensive options. Some libraries may not have the money to acquire an electronic version of a resource they purchased years ago in print or microform. Other libraries are bursting at the seams and can no longer effectively house their collections of the printed word; and thus digital materials become very attractive. Off-site storage facilities are one option for bulging stacks, but at the cost of removing potentially important resources from being found by a student or historian browsing the shelves. In order for both librarians and historians to have more informed discussions on the research and teaching needs of historians, and the budget and space realities faced by librarians, this book will hopefully provide enough information to provide a common ground for discussion.

The author is not so presumptuous to believe this book to be the final word on the subject but instead offers this as a means of encouraging librarians and historians to have a more informed discourse. The fruits of this dialogue will hopefully help both groups do their respective jobs in a way that truly advances the research and teaching within the discipline of history. In this respect, both librarians and historians are thus "Clio's helpers," after the Greek muse of history. The advice in this book is based on what the author learned while working on advanced degrees in both history and librarianship, as well as more than a decade of experience as a liaison, selector, reference, and instruction librarian for history (among other areas) at an ARL library.

Although one name as author of this book will appear in the metadata of the catalog record, no book such as this is completely the creation of a single person. The author would first like to thank his family for believing and for the encouragement and support during some very difficult times and personal crises. To my wife, colleague, best friend, and number one editor, Pixey Anne Mosley, a mere "thanks" cannot suffice for all the help and support you have given me over the years. Second, thanks go out to all the history faculty under whom I have studied or with whom I worked as student, graduate assistant, and colleague at Birmingham-Southern College, University of Alabama at Birmingham, University of Arkansas, and Texas A&M University. Where would I be without librarians and paraprofessional staff? Many thanks go out to all my colleagues, mentors, and those who helped me as a struggling student or a newly minted MLS at these institutions. One librarian needs a special thank-you for suggesting a new career direction at a critical time: Beth Juhl of the Mullins Library at the University of Arkansas. A very special thank-you goes to Dr. Margaret S. Dalton of the School of Library and Information Studies at the The University of Alabama. A historian in her own right, through her scholarship, teaching, advice, and mentoring, she did more than can be credited here to help the author in his success. Mr. Bill Page is one of the extremely talented and dedicated staff members at the Texas A&M University Libraries, and his creativity, insight, historical curiosity, and outright tenacity have made my work much easier. Many of my colleagues, both at the Texas A&M University Libraries, as well as fellow librarians at other institutions across the country, have also contributed in their own fashion (sometimes without knowing, when occasionally the author failed to realize the significance of an offhand comment until much, much later): ¡mil gracias a todos!

1

OVERVIEW OF HISTORY

Because history coursework is often part of basic education core curricula from middle school on into college, many librarians see the discipline as simple and straightforward: one of concrete and immutable facts about events, select people, and places. However, the perspective of historians working in higher education as their specialization is very different. For them, history is a complex and changing field with numerous subtleties and specializations. Historiography, or the study of how history is researched, written, and taught, is generally a required course for an advanced degree in the discipline, and is the genesis for many debates within the profession about the direction it is (or should be) taking. This chapter will introduce you to a better understanding of the more fascinating side of history.

BRIEF HISTORY OF HISTORY

What is history? What do historians do when they do history? What types of resources do they need? It was not so long ago that the answers to these questions would be very different from the answers here in the beginning of the twenty-first century. The discipline of history is very old, going back to the dawn of civilization. From the earliest societies to the present day there was recognition that certain members of a given society should be tasked with keeping that society's collective memory alive and accessible. The ancient Greeks thought history of such importance that they assigned Clio, one of the muses from their mythology, as patroness of the field. History was the glorious tales of the deeds (usually military) of great men or powerful institutions handed down through the generations, initially by word of mouth and only much later written out and printed in books. These histories, which offered little in the way of critical examination, were the most common methodology and practice until the mid-nineteenth century. During this period, new theories and practices developed as part of a larger movement toward making education more scientific and academically rigorous. In the field of history, one of the leading reformers in the 1800s calling for more empirical and professional practices was German scholar Leopold von Ranke. His theories demanded that scholars base historical research on sources created at the time period under examination, and then critically analyze the sources and write the histories as they happened, as opposed to merely repeating the stories most educated people already knew. These theories have guided generations of historians since (Novick 1988).

In the years following von Ranke, historians' methodologies and topics for research changed relatively little: grand narratives of great men based on their own writings as well as contemporary writings formed the bulk of history as it was researched, written, and taught. Modern critics dismiss many of the histories written in the nineteenth and early twentieth centuries as little more than hero-worship. Certain cherished myths regarding the honesty, wisdom, faith, and military prowess of the founding fathers of the United States date from this time. Likewise, writings from this time period generally made assumptions based on races and cultures that modern scholarship no longer accepts as valid, such as the assumed superiority of Western civilizations over those in other parts of the world. Similarly, writings from this time period, although based on primary sources, rarely offered the close critique most modern historians apply to both their subjects as well as their sources (Iggers 1993). Despite the shortcomings, the discipline was beginning to professionalize and mature, and a number of important historians lived and wrote during this time. Chapter 2 goes into this professionalization in more detail.

History is often the story of change and the discipline itself began to experience dramatic changes around the mid-twentieth century. The latter half of the twentieth century and the early years of the twenty-first century have witnessed dramatic changes and challenges to the grand narrative style of history as well as the subjects historians have explored. These new challenges and changes asked different questions that required new primary source materials as well as looking at the known primary sources in new ways. The turmoil of the civil rights era brought more questions about the way history was used to explain or defend a past many scholars began to see as racist and oppressive. Not just race, but members of the lower socioeconomic classes began to be examined as many in academia began a serious critique of the capitalist system using theories first proposed by Karl Marx. With the chaos, uncertainty, and crisis raised by the Vietnam War, many historians turned their critical examinations to the actions of the U.S. government and its motivations. New methodologies from other disciplines within the social sciences were modified to better shine light on the past. With the sexual revolution of the 1970s, historians began to examine the roles and contributions of women and to consider gender more frequently in their examination of the past. The upheavals society experienced carried over into higher education, inspiring serious reexaminations of the past, both in terms of the subjects of study (whereas before most histories concentrated on societal elites, afterward "history from below" became the norm), and in terms of methodology (historians began to borrow methods and sources from other disciplines). As a result of these changes, the discipline of history became much more interdisciplinary than many who do not keep up with the field for a living may realize (Iggers 1993). We librarians would like to think we kept up with these sea changes, but did we (or our predecessors during this time period) really do as well as we think? Each library will have a different answer. To answer this question, you must look at both the collection as well as the services your library offers to those who use it.

MAJOR FIELDS WITHIN HISTORY

History of *Everything*?

Everything has a history and herein lies a major problem, confounding even seasoned librarians. Even if history is *everything*, does that mean we really need to collect it? Prior to the mid-twentieth century, historical research and writing primarily limited itself to politics, diplomacy, and military history. There were decided tendencies to focus on Western civilizations, and to view the United States in isolation from other nations and events. For much of the twentieth century, written histories concentrated on the actions of those whom many modern critics dismiss as "great white men." However, that has thankfully changed and historians' publications now much more resemble everyday society, although some complain that their choice of topics and use of jargon has severely limited their appeal with a wider reading public. Current historiography takes a much broader view and frequently goes beyond national and international boundaries. Even American history is being placed in a larger, global context rather than in a vacuum, disconnected from ideas and influences in other continents. While politics and economics at the local, national, and international levels are still important as subjects, historians have been busily probing other topics as well. The efforts of the recent generations of historians have resulted in an explosion in the output of historical writings on every topic imaginable. Practically any area can be fertile ground for serious inquiry by current historical researchers. Many academic historians now address issues surrounding social and cultural studies as well as the traditional fields of political, diplomatic, and military histories. In addition to the history of times and places, countries, or regions, the histories of societal components (including groups based on race, ethnicity, gender, or socioeconomic class) or societal activities are crossing discipline boundaries on a daily basis and coming under the scrutiny of the historian's lens. This presents challenges for libraries as it makes the classification of a history book much more difficult to define.

Defining a Specialization or Focus

Historians define themselves in a variety of ways. One of the most obvious is by the geographical location of their primary field of research (e.g., a historian of the American South, or a historian of British colonialism). Generally, they will further specify a time period (medieval, eighteenth century, Han dynasty). Other historians define themselves by different criteria and can complicate things as they claim to study areas such as technology or religion. Two of the more recent trends, which can be difficult to pin down, are the Atlantic World and Comparative Borders. Atlantic World historians typically look at the myriad types of relations between the major players of the Triangle Trade (i.e., the European imperial powers of Spain, France, Great Britain, and others; the New World colonies of North, Central, and South America; and the western coasts of Africa). Examples of important topics for Atlantic World historians' research include these areas:

- Effects of the Atlantic slave trade
- Diasporas of African, Jewish, and other cultures throughout the area
- Interactions with indigenous populations
- Comparing gender roles on the frontier to those of the home country
- Relations between the colonizers and the colonists

This is not by any means a conclusive list. An intellectual historian researching the flow of ideas on social welfare between the United States and Europe in the early twentieth century could make a legitimate claim to be an Atlantic World specialist. Comparative Borders can be even broader than Atlantic World, as a border is frequently defined as any point where two or more cultural groups meet and interact. This meeting point could be a physical, geographic area, or it could be more abstract and metaphorical (including but not limited to race, class, and gender). Just as there are borders separating nations, there are also sexual/gender borders, racial and ethnic borders, religious borders, architectural borders, literary borders (or study of the literature from a specific geographical border), and more. Sometimes the interaction is peaceful and profitable as the parties form trading relationships with each other. However, violence is not uncommon and Comparative Border historians may also examine issues relating to conquest, domination, assimilation, and discrimination. Learning what a particular historical research term means is one of the first points to being able to assist library patrons in that area (Ritter 1993).

MAJOR RESEARCH METHODS USED

The old image of a solitary historian poring over a dusty tome or a forgotten diary in a darkened archive is still every bit as valid today. The written word, whether contained in diaries, correspondence, a bound codex, microfilm newspaper, or scanned digital image, is the basis for their analysis of what happened and why. While some of these sources are now available in an electronic format, many more are not. Historians look to what was written or said in the past to answer their questions. Their conclusions are based on what can be found in these old documents. How did Thomas Jefferson reconcile his ideas of individual freedom with his owning slaves? A historian seeking an answer to this question would probably start by looking at the surviving materials Jefferson himself actually wrote. Likewise, agricultural census records for specific years may show how a community survived or failed during the Dust Bowl era. Text preserved on English pipe rolls, a type of scroll, would tell a historian about society and taxation during the medieval period. German prayer books from the times of the Protestant Reformation may hold clues about how the warring sides felt about their adversaries. Finally, even advertisements in newspapers and magazines from earlier times can speak volumes about gender roles and racial stereotypes and the way these were accepted by popular culture of the time.

By engaging these old sources (generally known as primary sources), historians can begin to piece together what people experienced and believed at the time. Using sources created at the time of and as close as possible to the events being investigated is of paramount importance to historians' work. They look for patterns, trends, or other important statements regarding their topic of investigation. They also use the later works of scholars such as themselves (also known as secondary sources) to set the old sources in proper historical context and explain the significance of the sources they are using and the events they are examining. Unlike some disciplines in the sciences where anything older than five years is generally deemed obsolete and undesirable, for historians, the definitive secondary source on a given topic may be forty or more years old. Frederick Jackson Turner presented his frontier thesis in 1893, yet modern-day historians of the American West still begin many discussions with some kind of reference to Turner. Historians of the American Southwest must still tip their figurative hats to Herbert Bolton, who founded the field in the early decades of the twentieth century. C. Vann Woodward's classic study of the Jim Crow South, written in the mid-1950s (in the midst of turbulent racial strife), still finds its way onto contemporary doctoral preliminary exam reading lists; while E. P. Thompson's classic work on the origins of England's working class is more than forty years old but is still read by the current generation of history students. Historians must acknowledge these critical works, despite their age, in their own writing as part of their literature review.

Current historians often supplement these practices with methodologies based on or borrowed from both the social sciences, including demographic statistics from the past, in addition to humanities tools such as literary criticism. These changes have opened up the discipline to examining previously underrepresented groups such as ethnic minorities, women, and the lower socioeconomic classes. Some historians may employ historical census statistics to examine the socioeconomic condition of immigrants within a specified geographical region. Others build upon the writings and theories of Michel Foucault or other cultural theorists and philosophers in their investigations on power and its uses and abuses within a given society. A few historians are also turning to certain sociological resources as they examine whiteness, or the perceived societal advantages one ethnic group has enjoyed over another simply because of skin color. Over the course of the past fifty years, historical inquiry has become more esoteric, but also more sophisticated and interdisciplinary, demanding more from resources and their analysis (Ritter 1993; Novick 1988).

USE AND CHARACTERISTICS OF PRIMARY AND SECONDARY SOURCES

As mentioned previously, sources created at the time of the event under investigation are called primary sources, primary documents, or original sources, and it is absolutely essential that a serious history scholar consult these resources. These sources are the evidence upon which historians rely as they build their argument and defend their thesis. As historian Robin Winks stated, "By a 'source' the historian means material that is contemporary to the events being examined. Such sources include, among other things, diaries, letters, newspapers, magazine articles, tape recordings, pictures, and maps" (Winks 1969). Primary sources can be any format or any age, and can fall under any call number, depending on the topic. An overview of representative formats of interest includes:

- Books (published at the time)
- Magazines
- Newspapers
- Diaries
- Government documents
- Manuscripts
- Photographs
- Microforms

Depending on the nature of the project and who the intended audience is, digital reproductions of any of the above formats may also be acceptable. However, since historians tend to be a skeptical bunch, most would rather use the original, or at least be able to compare the original to the digital copy for veracity, as scanning resolution can be a factor on older materials with faint, spidery script. It happens that some projects to scan and digitize microfilm newspapers do not execute the scan at a resolution high enough to permit adequate enlargement or easy readability. On these occasions, the microfilm original must be consulted, and perhaps rescanned at a higher resolution in order for the historian to make use of it. Your library (whether it is the interlibrary loan department or other) must be willing to handle such requests. Similarly, if a microfilm was poorly made or has been badly scratched over the years, it may be beyond the ability of scanning and digital cleanup to render a salvageable image. Since the scans may be of documents several hundred years old and may be subjected to optical character recognition software (OCR), certain archaic type characters used in printing of the time may confuse the computer and render text that bears little resemblance to the original. And of course, if the historian is trying to decipher handwritten documents from a previous century, OCR may be worse than useless. Improvements are being made, but general practice has yet to perfectly reproduce the original document completely.

What defines a source as being primary is its proximity to the event or time period under investigation. Historians will want sources by someone personally involved or as close to the event as possible; hence the preference for diaries, letters, or other documents created at the time and by those involved. Depending on the topic, a source need not be old to be primary; a newspaper from the Vietnam War era is as valid to a historian interested in the events of those pivotal times as a book printed by Gutenberg himself would be to a historian who works in that era. Secondary sources are scholarly works written and published after the fact. These include the scholarly monographs, edited works, and journal articles that fill the shelves of many a library. Secondary sources are important for historians because these sources help build the context around the main topic of interest, provide background on prior investigations, and set the intellectual foundation upon which the historian builds his or her argument. A scholarly secondary source is especially prized if it has an extensive bibliography that leads to primary sources previously unknown to the researcher, or even to related secondary works offering different perspectives (Kitchens 2001). You can find more discussion on primary and secondary sources in later chapters on instruction and reference services.

SCHOLARLY PRODUCTION: BOOKS, BOOK REVIEWS, MORE BOOKS, SCHOLARLY ARTICLES, AND MORE BOOKS!

Although there are other important forms that should be considered as well, the scholarly monograph serves as the chief form of scholarly communication for historians. Historian and librarian Margaret F. Stieg has noted that scholarly monographs hold primacy of place for scholarly output. Historians write books and are often as proud of their prose as of their research skills. Tenure requirements at many research universities involve converting one's dissertation into a polished monograph, preferably published by a respected university press. For further promotions at research universities, additional monograph publications are expected. There is a legitimate reason for this emphasis on book-length publications. The monograph provides the historian with enough room to make as complete an argument as possible, using a wide range of sources, and placing it within the context both of the times of the events and of previous research. Historians are judged by their peers based on their ability to do exhaustive research and formulate persuasive arguments based on the sources they find (Stieg 1986).

Another key scholarship tool for historians is the book review. Stieg believes reviews of books are important, as through reviews historians comment on work done by their peers. The book reviews that appear in scholarly historical journals are not brief summaries, but critical and detailed assessments that provide an opportunity for discourse and commentary on the quality of research and writing in the profession. Some reviews are multipage, critical works that appear more like articles than the reviews normally seen on books in librarianship. These reviews are an excellent method for historians (and history librarians) to keep up with emerging scholarship in the field. One caveat regarding book reviews in major academic journals in history is that the reviews often appear a year or more after the book was published. Subject specialist librarians should be aware that reviews can be slow to appear and should not take it amiss if they cannot find a review for a recently published title (Stieg 1986).

Historians also generate scholarly articles and presentations. Articles in scholarly journals provide a place for new theories or core ideas for future monographs to be tried out before a professional audience. The same could be said for the scholarly communication that takes place at professional conferences, where the papers presented often represent the seeds for the presenter's latest research idea. In this information age based on the Internet, historians use the many H-Net listservs to maintain communication with each other, as is discussed in more detail in a later chapter. Being able to communicate with fellow experts in their fields is also important to practicing scholars.

The concerns for libraries and librarians should be obvious. Dalton and Charnigo refer to historians' desire for materials in their fields, especially books, as "insatiable" (Dalton and Charnigo 2004). Many historians utilize social science resources and selected methodologies; nevertheless, like other humanities disciplines, the monograph remains vitally important. Despite the advent of new electronic forms of disseminating information, books (whether print or digital) are still libraries' stock-in-trade for historians. Because history is a very book-heavy, library-intensive discipline, it is absolutely crucial that librarians in all departments are aware of what historians need and be equally sensitive to the manner in which they use library materials. Historians need to be able to closely read a book's text; they will dissect the argument and challenge the sources upon which it is built. Lightly skimming through as one generally does the latest best-seller on a Kindle, Nook, iPad, or other e-reader is not generally acceptable. While e-books hold some advantages for libraries, including not having to use a physical object, easy searchability, and availability at all hours; these advantages are generally lost on historians, who must scrutinize in detail the author's thesis and use of evidence (the sources) as they flip back and forth between text and endnotes. Although subject to change in future versions, footnotes and endnotes can be particularly difficult to use in some e-book formats. Historians need not be given a blank check, however, and library resources must be allocated in a logical and equitable fashion based on the primary mission of the institution, but librarians must never forget that the library is to the historian what the laboratory is to the chemist (AHA 2000; Delgadillo and Lynch 1999).

EMERGING AREAS

As mentioned earlier, the discipline of history has witnessed a sea change in the last half of the twentieth century as previously ignored or underrepresented groups have been given more of a historical voice. The efforts of the recent generations of historians have resulted in an explosion in the output of historical writings on every topic imaginable. This is demonstrated by looking at a sample representation of highly contrasting research topics found in a typical academic history department, all fertile ground for serious inquiry by current scholars:

- History of changes in office telecommunications
- Antebellum lifestyles of poor, non-slave-holding, white farmers
- World War I veterans' affairs in Europe
- Victorian-era criminal justice in Ireland
- Eighteenth-century social interactions in China's urban areas
- Visitors to the Spanish missions in the American Southwest in the early twentieth century
- Foreign medical exchange programs between the two world wars
- Islamic cultural practices and religious ritual during the early Middle Ages
- Encounters between Native Americans and Europeans in the American South
- Twelfth-century clashes between Europeans and Muslims

It is a daunting task to try and keep tabs on where the discipline will go next. Specialists in American history are looking beyond what has commonly been accepted as American to take a more global consideration of both American influence abroad as well as foreign influence on America. The previously mentioned fields of Comparative Borders and Atlantic World offer wide opportunities to research a variety of esoteric topics such as female street food vendors of the American Southwest in the late nineteenth and early twentieth centuries, or foodways as examples of cultural persistence and appropriation. Research into issues of identity formation among indigenous populations and their persistence in the face of domination by outside colonial powers can find fertile ground in almost any geographical locale and chronological period, as for example the formation of Indian nationalism during the British colonial era. The diasporas resulting from the slave trade have led to recent studies in African populations and traditions in the Caribbean as well as Central and South America. Women and gender roles in myriad times and places continue to be perennially popular topics. Related to gender issues is a growing attention paid to male sexuality and homosexuality across time and space.

History librarians, particularly if new to subject responsibilities in this field, would do well to peruse several recent issues of the *American Historical Review*, which is available in JSTOR (http://www.jstor.org). This is the scholarly publication of the American Historical Association (AHA), which (despite the name) is not just for historians specializing in American history, but rather historians regardless of specialty living in the United States who want to keep up with the profession. Emerging trends often find their way into forums, articles, or feature reviews in this important journal. Additional journals new subject specialists may wish to examine include the *Journal of World History*, and *Reviews in American History*, both of which are available through the Project MUSE database (http://muse.jhu.edu).

OVERLAP WITH OTHER AREAS IN THE LIBRARY

As stated earlier, everything has a history, which can cause some confusion, in all aspects of library services and collection building. In large libraries, the selector for history and the selector for women's studies may be two different people with different ideas about what a history of women's studies book should look like and who should buy it. At a school with important engineering programs, a class on the history of the space program or automobile may be one of the most popular course offerings in the department, which needs historical technical resources for student term papers. Who would teach the library skills session for this class: the history librarian or the engineering librarian? Even small libraries or those with overtaxed budgets will need to think carefully about how they define *history* for collection purposes so that resources can be allocated most effectively. How does one librarian keep track of everyone's needs when they are all over the historical map? Does a monograph of criminal justice during the Victorian era in County Kent qualify as British history (LCCN DA), criminology (LCCN HV), or British law (LCCN KD)? If the local British historian wants the library to purchase such a book, which librarian handles the request? What if the interested reader is from the sociology department? These are all issues that the history librarian will need to consider and discuss with peer subject librarians to make sure needed titles are acquired, but not duplicated. These issues are discussed in more detail in chapters 6 and 7.

Besides supporting the history department research and teaching initiatives, new subject specialist librarians for history should be aware that scholars in other disciplines may have an interest in history as it relates to their specialty. Thus, a professor in the communications department may have research and teaching interests in presidential campaign rhetoric from the nineteenth century. A graduate student in biology may arrive at the reference desk looking for sources on breeding methods for dairy cattle from the early twentieth century. A physicist may be working on a biography of Sir Isaac Newton. Likewise, who is going to explain to Dr. Schmidt in engineering that the German-language engineering journals from the 1930s he is using for his research on Adolf Hitler's synthetic fuels programs are scheduled to be moved to remote storage . . . the engineering librarian or the history librarian? None of these scholars teach history courses or may otherwise be affiliated with the history department, yet all are engaged in historical research, which you, the history subject specialist librarian, may be called upon to support. Often resources to support these interdisciplinary areas will fall outside the traditional LC call numbers C–F (or Dewey 900). Librarians must recognize their responsibility to meet educational and research needs in any area and negotiate with peers when appropriate.

Most often, history intersects with related humanities and social science disciplines such as the following:

- American studies
- English
- Foreign languages and cultures
- Cultural geography
- Religion
- Political science
- Economics
- International relations
- Genealogy studies
- Cultural anthropology/archaeology
- Race and ethnic studies
- Regional studies programs
- Art/architecture
- Sociology

However, history can also intersect with selected hard and applied sciences such as biology, chemistry, engineering, and physics. The best solution is often the simplest and librarians need the freedom to work and make decisions for whatever call number needed materials require without being constrained by artificial barriers that slow the acquisition of necessary resources. Additionally, librarians should be able to communicate with each other in a collegial manner that facilitates collaboration and cooperation (Hickey and Arlen 2002; Kitchens, Mosley, Marner, and Highsmith 2002; Metz and Foltin 1990). In this model, each librarian contributes pieces of specialized knowledge to a greater whole that combines historical research techniques and methodology to the topical knowledge of the discipline's librarians.

CONCLUSION

In wrapping up, there are several key points to be aware of when serving as the history subject specialist librarian. Everything has a history, and this creates numerous opportunities and challenges for librarians trying to serve historians and their students as their primary clientele. As the discipline evolves and continues to mature, new areas will be opened for investigation, new sources will be required, and new students will need to be taught research skills (even if it is applying old skills to new, digital formats). To better manage these new challenges, history librarians will need to keep up with the new trends in historical scholarship, as well as new tools and resources offered, or even new upgrades and changes to interfaces of existing resources. Librarians will need to be aware how decisions made about a particular set of sources or journal may have repercussions beyond the most obvious, immediate users. As historians and the students they teach cast their nets far and wide in the quest for more sources on their topics, the topics are going far beyond the old, traditional histories of dead presidents and forgotten battles. The discipline has changed to research previously underrepresented groups such as women and minorities. The focus in topics for historical research has shifted from the centers of power and seats of government to those on the fringes and margins of society. Librarians must be ready with the knowledge and resources that will allow historians and their students to access the necessary information in myriad formats, from digital to parchment, from the printed word to statistics, from any time and any place in the world.

2
___

LEARNING YOUR NEW LANDSCAPE

The first chapter introduced you to the discipline of history. This chapter will help you construct your own knowledge base and build connections with peer knowledge resources. Sometimes the required resources of historians have special considerations that create challenges for researchers and the librarians who try to assist them. Familiarizing yourself with the resource issues that historians face, the better-known names and interpretations within the profession, and some of the paths to self-education will help you appreciate the scope of your new role as history librarian.

MATERIALS NEEDED

A more thorough discussion of resources and concomitant issues will be found in chapter 6. However, here are some important, foundational considerations new history librarians need to know up front. While the topics for research and teaching have opened up considerably, history remains a discipline heavily dependent on the written word. Historians are arguably the heaviest users of library materials (especially monographs); the library really is their laboratory. History is a conversation the present has with the past for the future, and thus sources created in the past that survive to the present are essential. The resources that historians are absolutely reliant upon, depending on the topic being examined, include (but are not limited to) the following:

- Books
- Personal manuscripts
- Correspondence
- Scholarly articles
- Ephemera (such as brochures and pamphlets)
- Popular magazines and newspapers of the time (including the advertisements)
- Official records from legislative bodies or similar institutions

- Government agricultural reports
- Supreme Court (state or federal) opinions
- Tax rolls
- Census data and demographic statistics
- Shipping manifests
- Maps (either from the time period studied or contemporary)
- Published sermons
- Primers or other educational materials for children
- Baptismal, marriage, and burial records
- Cookbooks
- Transportation schedules
- Patents
- Corporate records
- Diplomatic communiqués

The resources needed are as varied as historians' interests. The questions the historian poses will go far in defining what sources are required for the answers. Also, in order to write convincingly and with authority, historians must consult huge quantities of these resources. A single news article from the *Times* (London) is not sufficient, but must be studied in context of what was said of the same event by other newspapers in London, or in papers from the other major political parties (since the *Times* has been a mouthpiece of the Conservative or Tory party for decades). Depending on the topic, this commentary might extend for days or weeks leading up to the event, or even for years afterward. In a librarian's world, these sources could realistically be anywhere in the collection regardless of call number: a historian researching the Franciscan missions in Texas ostensibly could find books in LCCN BR and BX (Christianity and Roman Catholicism), F (North America, Local History, Texas and Mexico), GT or GV (Manners and Customs, and Recreation—as these missions are tourist attractions), H (Social Sciences, including Land Use and Social History), and NA (Architecture); not just DP (Spain) and E (Americas; which could be further subdivided into Indians, Discovery, and Elements of the Population).

Just as the nature and topics of historical research have changed, so too have the formats of these materials historians use in their quest to unlock the mysteries of the past. Prior to the twenty-first century, most materials historians used were printed, either in books, journals, or archival manuscripts. In the second half of the twentieth century, microtext (microfilm, microfiche, and microcard—or micro-opaques) allowed the dissemination of rare materials to libraries that could afford to purchase these materials and maintain the equipment to enlarge and read them. Microfilm allowed newspapers to be preserved in an archival manner that would last decades longer than the fragile newsprint. Now in the early years of the twenty-first century, many materials and resources of interest to historians are becoming available digitally as private companies and some public entities have initiated projects to scan documents and make them accessible through a Web-browsing interface or in an institutional repository. This allows users to be either a few hundred yards or even a few hundred miles from the document's physical location. Also, a researcher can search thousands of documents for relevant keywords and phrases at once and download or print the results with relative ease. Even the old microform has a new lease as some newer readers now allow end users to scan needed pages and save them to a portable memory device. While some futurists in our profession are quick to proclaim the death and burial of microtext, libraries of all kinds (public, community colleges, even research universities) must continue to maintain and service high-quality microtext reader/printer/scanners. Advances in technology have brought the prices down in recent years. The requirement for these machines continues because some locally produced microfilm may never be digitized for copyright or other simple economic reasons. Similarly, some materials requested via interlibrary loan will come in microtext format. Finally, there are many microtext collections that are not attractive candidates for scanning by companies such as ProQuest or Gale/Cengage since they will not be able to recoup their costs in subscription sales. However, regardless of format, digital or analog, the text, its context, and provenance are all vitally important to historians' research.

WHAT IS AND MAY NOT BE AVAILABLE (THE TRUTH IS *NOT* ALWAYS OUT THERE)

Because historical research is based upon the collected material of the time being investigated, it is reliant on the people of the time seeing the information being worth collecting, saving, and sharing, for future generations. Consequently, because not all information was valued enough to preserve at the time, there may be questions where the information is not readily available to a particular library or in an easy-to-use format, if it even exists at all. Many historical resources have been destroyed in natural disasters (flood, earthquake, etc.), have been burned (sometimes intentionally, other times accidentally), remain classified by security agencies, are housed in closed collections with restricted access, or exist in archives across the sea. In January of 1920, a fire at the Commerce Building destroyed all but a few fragments of the 1890 U.S. population census, much to the vexation of untold numbers of future researchers (http://www.archives.gov/research/census/1890/1890.html).

Although the U.S. government has a program to declassify documents and information no longer considered sensitive, and a large number are electronically available via a commercial database from Cengage/Gale, even these are not completely free from secrecy. Even though declassified and available to researchers, some of these documents have been further sanitized, which means material still considered sensitive is blacked out. Also, there are still many more materials that have not yet been reviewed for declassification. Historians looking for resources of the late Cold War period may be very disappointed in how little material is currently available. Researchers looking for information on the Taliban and the terrorist attacks of September 11, 2001, are even more likely to come up empty-handed. Requests made through the Freedom of Information Act (FOIA) often take an exasperating period of time to work their way through the bureaucratic channels. The age of electronic information has only complicated matters as debates and lawsuits have raged over what constituted official e-mail from elected officials, whether these e-mails were considered worth preserving, and in what format. While we in the United States have certain expectations regarding the openness of our government's records, other countries have different standards. Librarians may be asked to help a historian track down whether a particular item to which the historian was denied access while overseas is somehow available for interlibrary loan from another library in North America.

There are also plenty of examples of data never collected at the time, but considered historically significant today (when someone asks you for original sources on Central European peasant holdings during the Renaissance broken down into hectares, you will appreciate this). Also, keep in mind that national borders and place names in many parts of the world have been fluid until very recently. While it seems trivial, not all resources have been corrected for these changes, such as the earlier Peking now being more faithfully rendered as Beijing. Think about the breakup of the old Soviet Union after the Cold War ended, and the new independent and quasi-independent states that surround Russia. In Africa, many nations are no longer known by the names imposed by their former colonizers, but have taken indigenous names more meaningful to the local population. Even in the United States, finding early materials on territories that later became states with different borders can sometimes be challenging and not always intuitive.

Early histories often reinforced the notion that the winners write the history books. Modern historians trying to balance this perspective sometimes discover inconvenient truths or other facts that the winners would rather remain hidden. History is, unfortunately, filled with graphic examples of man's inhumanity to man, and this puts some novice historians off of the subject and offends people who may identify with a particular group that committed some atrocity long ago. The USC Shoah Foundation Institute for Visual History and Education, currently housed on the campus of the University of Southern California, has collected more than 50,000 videotaped testimonies of survivors of the Nazi Holocaust. These testimonies, available to historians through subscribing libraries and museums, offer invaluable (but sometimes graphic) firsthand accounts for historians researching that tragedy (http://dornsife.usc.edu/vhi). Books on the Armenian genocide of the early 1900s or on the tragedy of lynching and other racial violence in the United States such as the gruesome *Without Sanctuary: Lynching Photography in America* may seem fit more for the horror section, but history cannot always be neat and pretty. Sometimes the material itself is shocking or offensive; sometimes it is actually the terms one has to use to find the material that can cause discomfort. Librarians as well as historical researchers need to remember language changes over time and in response to societal mores. In earlier times, euphemisms were sometimes used for sexual references, but the search engines behind primary source databases cannot always comprehend the intended message. Hence, if a researcher is looking for examples of late nineteenth-century prostitution in a database of digital newspapers, the librarian assisting should know that sometimes instead of mentioning *prostitute*, the newspaper would probably use terms such as *soiled doves* or *unfortunate girls*. In other cases, earlier terms that defined racial, ethnic, or characteristics of national origin are now recognized as demeaning and inappropriate. This is especially true for historians working on immigrant communities in the United States, or the oppressive and sometimes violent response to immigration from Asia and Central Europe in the late nineteenth and early twentieth centuries. Newspaper articles of the time often used epithets modern society considers offensive to describe immigrants from China, Mexico, Bohemia, and Italy. Researchers and librarians assisting them with these types of topics may have to come to terms with the racist past, move out of their comfort zone, and think in terms of the language of the times, places, and cultures that created the sources to locate and interpret these primary sources appropriately without losing their sensitivity to the current view of these terms as offensive.

MAJOR HISTORIANS AND THEIR EVOLVING METHODOLOGIES

There have been a number of important historians through the ages, but most current historiography (a critical study of how history has been written about over the years) concentrates upon historians from the 1800s to the present. Although a thorough discussion of important historians would require a complete monograph in itself, what follows is a brief mention of a few of the more prominent names in historiography. German scholar Leopold von Ranke is often considered the first professional historian in the modern sense of the term. His rigorous and critical readings of sources created at the time of events established the basic methodology that all scholarly historians have followed since. Frenchmen Fernand Braudel, Lucien Febvre, and Marc Bloch offered a new interpretation of history just prior to and after World War II with what is often called the *Annales* school after their journal. This interpretation of history looks beyond great men to the subtle changes in the land, climate, economic patterns, and societies over the courses of centuries (the *longue durée*) rather than short, pivotal events such as a single battle or even an individual's life. Braudel, for example, traced economic changes over the course of several centuries in early modern European states along the Mediterranean; these changes eventually evolved into capitalism. The 1982 movie, *The Return of Martin Guerre*, with its extremely graphic historical realism, brought social history into the popular eye; and Princeton University professor Natalie Zemon Davis, having written the book on which the movie was based, became one of the best-known social historians as a result. In Great Britain, E. P. Thompson and Eric Hobsbawm created a stir when they applied Marxist theories to explain the effects of the Industrial Revolution and the origins of the English working class. Contemporary historians, reflecting the influence of cultural studies, often employ theories formulated by scholars Edward Said, Michel Foucault, and Antonio Gramsci as they investigate power (or hegemony) relations among cultures in a myriad of times and places (Iggers 1993).

In the United States, there have been a number of influential historians and their schools. For much of the nineteenth century, writers of American history did not take a very critical approach. What was written consisted more of celebration and myths, such as those perpetrated by Parson Weems (George Washington and the cherry tree) and other amateurs that passed as history. However, with the founding of the American Historical Association in 1884 and a drive to make historical research more rigorous and scientific in nature, the discipline changed and became more demanding. Von Ranke's ideas of critically reading the primary sources took hold and became the new standard (Novick 1988).

For many in the United States, American history begins at Plymouth Rock. Historian Perry Miller's Puritans, committed to their "errand into the wilderness," founded a "city on a hill" and struggled to maintain their faith in a strange, new world. His work set the standard for years and is still read by graduate students. Later historians of the area would take markedly different approaches from Miller's concentration on Puritan elites, as Laurel Thatcher Ulrich did in her 1991 Pulitzer Prize-winning winning book on a New England midwife, thus offering new insights on a segment of the population regularly ignored by earlier generations of historians. The *Mayflower's* landfall in 1620 certainly marked English colonization of North America in earnest, but other European powers, including Spain, France, and the Netherlands were also busy staking claims to portions of the continent. James Axtell and Colin Calloway are but two recent historians to examine other nations' colonial efforts in what is now the Northeastern United States.

At the 1893 Chicago World's Fair, Frederick Jackson Turner espoused his "frontier thesis," in which he discussed the Anglo expansion onto the American frontier, its role in the development of American identity, and the repercussions of its closure. Historians of the American West and Borderlands have had to address Turner's work ever since. Herbert E. Bolton, a student of Turner's, offered a different take on early American history by focusing his attention on the Borderlands and Spanish expansion north from Mexico into the entire southern third of the modern United States. Bolton's work showed the need for American historians to consider the Spanish roots in the Southwestern United States as an important part of the nation's history. Contemporary historians of the American West, such as Howard Lamar, Patricia Nelson Limerick, and the late David J. Weber, are noted for their expansion of historical understanding beyond Turner and Bolton, and their inclusion of additional races and industries to the earlier sagas of cowboys, cattle drives, and hostile Native Americans.

Heated debate by historians on the causes and effects of the Civil War and Reconstruction Era began shortly after the actual shooting ended. At the close of the nineteenth century, William A. Dunning and his students from Columbia University churned out scathing and often racist polemics deriding the North's harsh treatment of the former Confederates. Later, twentieth-century revisionist historians such as C. Vann Woodward, Carl Degler, John Hope Franklin, and Columbia historian Eric Foner have offered a more balanced view of that turbulent period, as well as of Southern history and African American history in general.

Charles and Mary Beard established what became the progressive school, as they wrote about the consequences of American industrialization, the harm done to the agrarian lifestyle, and attempts at reform in the late nineteenth century. Conversely, the next generation of historians, Richard Hofstadter among them, who wrote in the era of McCarthy's redbaiting, established the consensus school. Consensus historians tended to look more at what united Americans and what they had in common, unlike their progressive predecessor, who emphasized divisive issues such as race and class and the shortcomings of the capitalist system. Diplomatic history can be just as divisive: New Left historians such as Walter LaFeber employ Marxist interpretations to critique American expansion as imperialism, while John Lewis Gaddis credits Ronald Reagan and the free enterprise, capitalist system of the United States with contributing to winning the Cold War.

A more detailed discussion of both world historiography and American historiography would rapidly expand beyond the scope of this monograph. Therefore, the best advice for you, as the history librarian, would be to talk with those using the collections about what resources are needed and where the balance should be. History faculty who teach historiography classes may have an interest in acquiring representative samples of various schools or interpretations; however, there may also be a need for scarce library resources to be used on other, more immediately relevant topic-specific materials or priorities. You can also find useful information by reading articles and book reviews in journals such as the *American Historical Review* (Bentley 1997; Boyd 1999; Iggers 1993; Ritter 1993).

CONTINUING EDUCATION

Unlike some disciplines, finding continuing education opportunities in history-related topics that would give one a better understanding at the big-picture level can be difficult. Obviously taking or auditing history courses at a local college or university may be one good way to increase your historical knowledge and awareness. Unfortunately, it may also be the most time-consuming and expensive. Additionally, introductory survey classes may not provide the depth of knowledge you may need to assist students at all levels or engage with faculty about their research, but auditing upper-level or graduate classes may require extensive background knowledge and an understanding of historical methodology to be effective.

Self-education with a few books recommended by colleagues or faculty members may be a more efficient use of time. You may want to start with Eric Foner's (1997) excellent work, *The New American History*. This book was explicitly intended and is especially useful for giving readers a thorough overview of the most important trends in American historical scholarship in the two decades prior to its publication in a single volume, and remains quite relevant despite its age. From a more international perspective, the first three chapter essays in Charles A. D'Aniello's *Teaching Bibliographic Skills in History* (1993) discuss the discipline as a whole. Despite the overall title, these initial essays in D'Aniello serve as an excellent introduction to the changes that have affected the discipline in the past fifty years and would give nonhistorian librarians a much better foundation to understand what historians are talking about, asking for, and why. New history librarians needing some ideas of what to teach in a library skills session would find the remainder of D'Aniello's book quite useful, as is covered in more detail in chapter 5. Finally, Peter Novick's *That Noble Dream* (1988) is often used as a textbook in graduate history classes to describe the nature of the profession in the United States, including some of the turbulent changes the field underwent in the closing decades of the twentieth century.

As presented in more detail in chapter 3, talking with history faculty over lunch or coffee is an excellent way to demonstrate a willingness to learn and work with them regarding their information needs. In return, they are often glad to share their knowledge and expertise. As a related area, many community colleges or local historical societies conduct workshops on family history/genealogy/local history that may prove insightful. Even if history subject specialists have no familial ties to the community in which they work, these opportunities can be useful in terms of awareness and knowledge of sources.

MENTORSHIP

Mentorship can come in many guises. Mentors can, perhaps, be most easily found in some of the library organizations mentioned below. However, subject specialist librarians for history can also find mentors within their local organizations or from outside. Even if you are the only librarian for history, your fellow librarians in some of the other, frequently related areas with interdisciplinary focus mentioned in chapter 1 can share their wisdom, sources, and assistance regarding general collection development procedures, reference tricks, and tips for successful bibliographic instruction sessions. Local history faculty can serve as subject-oriented mentors as well, and many an effective relationship can be built by getting out and talking with people. However, some librarians may be bothered with the prospects of being a novice history apprentice and still having to provide the expert level of service expected of librarians. To understand genealogical issues, a local public librarian or museum director may be an effective mentor to seek out.

One important aspect in seeking out a mentor is having a clear picture of what one hopes to get from the mentoring relationship. For example, it is important to recognize if one is seeking a mentor for knowledge of history (knowledge of the discipline), or for historical knowledge (knowledge of the subject), or for knowledge in librarianship (knowledge in how to be a better librarian) that just happens to be in a particular subject area. The answer to this question will help guide one to an appropriate mentor. If you believe the librarian for English or the religious studies librarian to be very good role models, you could ask either of them to mentor you in librarianship. For historical knowledge, turning to an undergraduate advisor, lecturer, or visiting assistant professor for assistance in learning the ropes of a new field may be less intimidating and create less blurring between your novice and expert roles than asking Distinguished Professor Roberts, who has published half a dozen books on very esoteric topics within the discipline. Also, as you interact with your new mentor, finding a common interest outside of, or tangentially related to, the subject can help build the connection and relationship.

LIBRARY ASSOCIATION DIVISIONS

Many subject specialist librarians, especially new ones, may be unsure where to begin and easily become overwhelmed by their new responsibilities. Help and mentoring is available and it is not difficult to find. Within ALA, the History Section of the Reference and User Services Association (RUSA) serves as one of the best places to make contacts with other history specialists. Most of the members are history bibliographers and the Historical Materials Committee from this section is responsible for reviewing the "Best Historical Materials" published annually in the journal *Reference and User Services Quarterly*. There is also the Instruction and Research Services Committee that can provide invaluable assistance for librarians wondering what to cover in information literacy programs in the field of history. For librarians seeking mentoring in local history or genealogy, there are RUSA History Section committees on each of those topics with fellow colleagues ready to help. The History Section also puts on a number of excellent programs and workshops at ALA conferences on genealogy and local history, which will give novices a jump-start on important materials in those popular areas. In addition to a regular conference meeting, the group often has a more relaxed dinner event at ALA conferences, which is a perfect way to meet professional peers from other institutions. For new history selectors with additional special interests or multidisciplinary responsibilities with a gender, ethnicity, or geographic focus, Association of College and Research Libraries (ACRL) has a number of sections that can open many opportunities and can be found at the following URL: http://www.ala.org/acrl/aboutacrl/directoryofleadership/sections.

- African American Studies (AFAS)
- Asian, African, and Middle Eastern (AAMES)
- Rare Books and Manuscripts (RBMS)
- Slavic and East European (SEES)

- Western European Studies (WESS)
- Women & Gender Studies (WSS)

Although none of these sections concentrate only on history, ours is a very interdisciplinary field and one should not be dissuaded simply because history is not explicitly mentioned in the section name. New selectors looking for opportunities to get involved and make connections are encouraged to attend program meetings and sign onto any e-mail lists. Contact information is generally located on the organization's website.

MAJOR HISTORICAL SOCIETIES AND ORGANIZATIONS

Just as the American Library Association has numerous divisions based on interest and specialization, there are numerous organizations and societies engaged in support of the research of history. One of the most important organizations that new librarians will need to be aware of is the American Historical Association (AHA), http://www.historians.org. Despite the name, the AHA is not just about United States history. Founded in 1884, it is the oldest professional organization in North America for historians of all specialties. Its journal, *The American Historical Review* (or *AHR*), is one of the most prestigious in the discipline. The AHA website and monthly newsletter, *Perspectives*, are excellent places to look for information about current issues within the discipline of history. For new history librarians looking for a single organization that pays attention to the histories of many different locales and time periods, the AHA and its publications certainly merit attention. In 1903, the Pacific Coast Branch of the AHA was founded. Information on the Pacific Coast Branch can be found at the URL http://pcb.cgu.edu. Historians in the western United States and Canadian provinces have their own journal and a separate conference meeting.

There are numerous niche scholarly societies and professional organizations for history. Indeed, some scholars have complained that the discipline has become too fragmented and suffers from overspecialization (Oshinsky 2000). History librarians may find themselves bewildered by the plethora of esoteric journals and groups. How would one keep track of them all? Actually tracking down contact and journal information for every organization is probably not a productive task considering that almost every state in the United States has a scholarly organization specializing in that state's history, plus various regional, national, and international organizations, as well as societies organized around a central topic. Depending on the size of the library and collection demands, librarians ought to at least keep up with their home state historical societies, plus any local societies that may exist, and they should know if the organizations support research in wider areas, such as regional or national societies. As discussed more in chapter 3, asking history faculty what associations they participate in, or looking at their published vitas on the departmental website, can give a sense of what organizations merit consideration. Fortunately for history selectors, the AHA's website has a page that lists more than 100 affiliated societies (state and local organizations are not included) with the corresponding website, contact information, and area of specialty. This page is a great asset to anyone trying to find a particular organization. Finally, it may also be worth a new history librarian's time to peruse the association websites of other scholarly organizations in some of the tangential fields of history, such as those of the American Studies Association, the Popular Culture Association/American Culture Association, and the Society of Architectural Historians.

ELECTRONIC DISCUSSION GROUPS

In this information age based on the Internet, many historians use the numerous H-Net listservs to maintain communication with each other. H-Net, short for Humanities Network, consists of almost 190 listservs on topics ranging widely from the Hapsburg Empire to American pop culture. While the main server has been hosted at Michigan State University for a number of years, the individual list editors are from all over North America and beyond. E-mail allows for the informal flow of communication among professional colleagues at schools around the nation or around the globe. Being able to communicate with fellow experts in their fields is also important to practicing scholars. Conference announcements, calls for papers, publishing opportunities, or questions about sources are frequently circulated to subscribers allowing members to keep up with one or more areas of interest. More information on subscribing to H-Net lists can be found at http://www.h-net.org. One caveat is that as a group, historians tend not to be too deep into the most current telecommunication technology or social networking. Not to say there are no historians twittering, blogging, or meeting with colleagues and students in Second Life, but generally, this community often lags behind other, more technologically oriented groups.

An opportunity to connect with fellow history bibliographers is the H-Net listserv, H-HistBibl, at http://www.h-net.org/~histbibl. Subscribers are history bibliographers from every part of librarianship: archives and special collections, cataloging and technical services, and reference and instruction. Although not an overly active or chatty listserv, calls for assistance rarely go unanswered. Messages are archived in a log going back to January 1999 so new members can look for previous discussions on a particular topic. In addition to H-HistBibl, selectors should feel free to sign up to any of the lists that look particularly useful or especially relevant to their collections. These are just two examples of methods for selectors to network and build a support group of colleagues to lean on when difficult issues arise. With the rise in popularity of blogs and wikis among many librarians, subject specialists may find other innovative means to connect with fellow bibliographers when help is needed.

CONFERENCES

In addition to ALA committee activities and conference programs mentioned in the previous section, there are other conference opportunities to establish connections with fellow librarians and history bibliographers. For librarians with extensive collection development responsibilities, the Annual Charleston Conference in Book and Serial Acquisitions, which takes place every November in Charleston, South Carolina, is an excellent and informative gathering for selectors to attend and network with professional colleagues. There, participants can go to programs and hear presentations on many of the most important issues facing acquisitions librarians today. Speakers and participants come from academic libraries, special libraries, corporations, publishing companies, and database vendors. The proceedings are currently being published by Libraries Unlimited Press, a division of Greenwood Publishing Group. Conference information can be found at the URL http://www.katina.info/conference. For librarians with more interests or responsibilities in bibliographic instruction and information literacy, LOEX (Library Orientation Exchange) is a nonprofit organization that acts as a clearinghouse for information on library instruction and information literacy. They hold an annual conference with published proceedings and have a quarterly publication with articles by practitioners. For more information, visit: http://www.emich.edu/public/loex/loex.html.

In getting to know the collection resources for which they are responsible as well as the local faculty who are actively researching and teaching in historical topics, it may be useful for librarians to attend historical conferences. Attending national, regional, and/or state historical conferences can greatly benefit new subject specialists by introducing them to the types of research that professional historians do and what they do with their results. If one cannot afford to attend the conference, one should read additional journals in history for the specific area and look at conference program topics for ideas. Librarians at public institutions, especially those in large, regional libraries, may find it useful to join regional associations if they have strong collections and interests in those areas (e.g., librarians in large public libraries in the Western states could find membership in the Western Historical Association, WHA, useful). The WHA website is currently located at the University of Missouri-St. Louis at http://www.westernhistoryassociation.org. Conversely, librarians in the Southeast might find membership in the Southern Historical Association, or SHA, very informative. The SHA website is located at the University of Georgia, http://www.uga.edu/sha. Similarly, there may be a need for genealogical support for local and regional historical materials. Besides U.S. regional historical associations, there are separate organizations of American historians who study international topics, such as the American Conference of Irish Studies and the World History Association, as well as learned societies overseas such as the Royal Historical Society of Great Britain, http://www.royalhistoricalsociety.org. Unfortunately, travel budgets are easy targets in times of economic crisis, and you may find yourself at an institution whose allocations for professional travel have been reduced. While ALA has begun using some virtual conference meetings, other organizations may not be as accommodating.

If you are fortunate enough to attend one, history conferences tend to be conducted very differently than library conferences. The exhibits will tend to be much smaller and quieter than one usually finds on the exhibit floor at even an ALA Mid-Winter Meeting. Exhibitors are usually publishers of scholarly works, reference works, and textbooks. There may also be some rare/out-of-print book dealers with booths as well. Large database companies offering significant primary source materials or other bibliographic services are beginning to discover these conferences, but it remains to be seen what the economic impact will be if they continue to attend. Instead of a full slate of discussion groups, organizational meetings, poster sessions, author signings, and book-truck drill teams, practically all sessions at a history conference are devoted to presenting new scholarly research. A session generally has a panel of three presenters, a moderator who introduces each speaker and keeps time, and an additional person to provide concluding commentary responding to the other speakers' presentations. Although some presenters will employ laptops and illustrations, many more will simply stand and read their papers. While librarians at ALA are accustomed to walking into and out of sessions in large rooms as they need in order to attend meetings, other presentations, or additional responsibilities, historical presentations tend to be in much smaller rooms with much fewer people in attendance. Those coming late or leaving early will be noticed as a distraction, although the practice of session-hopping is occurring more frequently.

Given that one may not have funds or may have just missed a conference opportunity, the best way for a librarian to get to know the local department is to talk with the history faculty and ascertain their needs for research and teaching, their impression of the library's collection, and their favorite sources, authors, and publishers, which will be discussed in more detail in chapter 3. In the meantime, librarians can request catalogs from publishers either via phone or e-mail, or they often can pick up the latest catalogs and speak directly with publishers' representatives in the exhibits area at conventions or professional organization meetings such as the ALA, ACRL, AHA, the OAH, SHA, and many others. Scholarly publishers and used-and-out-of-print book dealers are frequent exhibitors at these conferences and it is a good way to see the latest scholarship or hear about upcoming releases. The information in the catalog is generally duplicated on the publisher's website and more experienced selectors may find it easier to go directly to these websites, although searching and browsing capabilities will vary greatly.

CONCLUSION

This chapter has been about helping history librarians, particularly those that are novices to the discipline, discover what will be required of them in assisting historians and their students in research, information literacy, and collection building. The nature of the historical profession requires its practitioners to use sources created in the past, sometimes the very distant past (in terms of chronology, physical distance, or both). Finding and using these types of resources brings a unique set of challenges with which history librarians must learn to work. Some materials may be in foreign languages, or formats that do not permit easy digitization. Sometimes the sources are nonexistent and substitutes and surrogates must be found. The changes in the historical discipline have opened new topics for investigation, which require new types of resources, some of which were not systematically preserved in decades past. Finding these, even with electronic tools such as WorldCat and Google Books, can be a daunting challenge.

The good news is that history librarians do not have to go it alone, as help and mentoring are available. New librarians can find mentors both within and outside their organization, if they will look and keep an open mind. History faculty will generally be glad to discuss issues and information needs with someone willing to ask them and genuinely listen to their response. Fellow librarians can offer excellent advice and assistance in everything from bibliographic instruction tips to learning the bureaucracy that permeates every organization. Mentors also are available outside one's home campus. Within ALA, both ACRL and RUSA have subsections that address the concerns and needs of history librarians. Although none have "history" in their names, several ACRL sections recognize history's value and new history librarians can find great assistance there for a wide variety of issues. Meanwhile, RUSA has an entire section devoted to history and within that section are committees for genealogy, local history, bibliographic instruction, and historical materials. Outside of librarianship are electronic e-mail lists, professional organizations, and conferences, all of which librarians are welcome to join and attend. Attending history conferences can give history librarians wonderful new insights on history and its professional practitioners. Finally, there is plenty of self-education to be done. A few key titles were mentioned earlier and for librarians committed to understanding their new clientele, it would greatly behoove them to take the time and closely read the recommended books. As novelist L. P. Hartley wrote, "The past is a foreign country; they do things differently there." Librarians new to history specialist responsibilities should educate themselves just as they would before traveling to any foreign land.

3

GETTING TO KNOW AND UNDERSTAND YOUR LOCAL AUDIENCE

The focus of this chapter is to offer insights on how to develop an understanding of the clientele you are now serving as the history librarian. While there is an implicit assumption you are serving in an academic setting, you may have secondary community support responsibilities in addition to the primary institutional environment. It goes without saying that a community or four-year college history department's demands on the library will significantly differ from that of a Carnegie I research university with an ARL (Association of Research Libraries) member library. Understanding these differences in needs will make you a better librarian by giving you insight and ideas to better serve those needing assistance and resources for teaching and research about historical topics.

TALKING TO THE ACADEMIC DEPARTMENT

Different libraries will have different procedures, models, and roles for library liaisons and librarians. Librarians new to history responsibilities will need to take a little time to transition to the new procedures and expectations. Even if you are an experienced librarian, you may find some enlightening information here. Techniques that worked sufficiently well from a science or social science perspective may or may not be as effective when assisting history faculty and students. Unlike many science faculty or engineering faculty, historians (generally speaking) do not tend to be at the cutting edge of telecommunication technology, and unlike business faculty, may not be satisfied with a simple executive summary and bullet-point list, without some explanation. At some libraries, subject specialists will have wide latitude in communicating with departments and faculty with intuitive, easy-to-understand procedures and reasonable expectations regarding bibliographic instruction record keeping, reference support, and acquisition of new materials. At other institutions, librarians may find their autonomy severely limited, even to the point of having all materials purchasing decisions resting outside the library (such as in the academic department chair's office—it does happen) or having to navigate Byzantine procedures through innumerable bureaucratic hoops for approval from a committee with little to no guidance. If you are new to your role, you may be following the footsteps of a talented colleague who left clear documentation of expectations and updated resources, such as finding guides and collection development policies. Alternately, you may find yourself in disorganized chaos or benign neglect where you are basically starting from scratch, although a blank slate can be your opportunity to put your own stamp on how things are done.

These scenarios are obviously extremes and most libraries fall somewhere in the middle. Regardless of your experience, you are encouraged to learn and to use the system in place to the utmost of its effectiveness and follow established guidelines regarding communication channels, instruction schedules, and buying materials. If you feel that the system does not meet the needs of the department, you should begin collecting various kinds of data to prove that a change needs to be considered. Subject specialist librarians that are new to an organization should recognize that they may be the junior partners, so to speak, and may not be able to immediately make the sweeping changes they believe will improve service by ditching all of the perceived inefficient and wasteful practices used in the past. On the other hand, we are, after all, professionals. Whenever possible, librarians should have a high level of independence and autonomy to do their jobs in the most effective manner they see fit as long as it serves communicated needs of both the history department (faculty and students) and the library. Any processes above the front-line level should focus on ensuring that library skills classes are taught when asked for, and supported in ways that do not undermine the educational objectives of the history faculty member teaching the course. These processes should also insure that materials purchased reflect the needs of the departments, and otherwise avoid creating barriers to the librarian's effectiveness in all aspects of their liaison responsibilities. There is no one best way to be a librarian. One set of practices may not be best in all, or even a majority, of circumstances. Being flexible should be one's goal or mantra.

MEETING FACULTY ON THEIR OWN TURF

So how do you talk to faculty members? Do they even want to see you? Wouldn't they all be in class teaching, or meeting with students? An optimal situation is when there is an opportunity for a librarian-to-librarian hand-off, with the outgoing, or interim, specialist librarian taking you around and introducing you to the faculty members. However, this is much more the exception rather than the norm. More often, your predecessor is long gone before you take on the new responsibilities, particularly if you were newly hired into the role of history librarian. If you do not feel comfortable leaving the security of the library building, walking the halls of the history department and meeting the faculty face-to-face in their offices, it may be easier to contact them first by phone or e-mail. Initial contacts with the history faculty, whether by telephone or e-mail, could be for a less formal meeting; set up an appointment to meet for coffee or lunch first. Keep things casual, but professional. Another method would be to arrange with the department head to be placed on the agenda of the first faculty meeting of the new semester, or the next one if your appointment has occurred midterm. You do not need to take more than a few minutes, just long enough to introduce yourself, pass out enough business cards for anyone who wants one, and list a few bullet points of what the library can offer, or inform them of new services or location changes for familiar services; the latter is especially useful at the first meeting of the semester if some policies, procedures, or renovations changed things over the summer. If information literacy is given strategic importance or emphasized by your institution, you will want to make sure interested faculty can get in touch with you to set up meeting times with their classes. Keep things brief for the first meeting. Thank the department head for giving you the opportunity to have a few minutes of the meeting, but remember they have other important business to attend and you are very much a guest; don't overstay your welcome. On the other hand, you want to give them enough information to whet their appetites and get them interested and thinking about what services the library has to offer and how your support could benefit their research and teaching.

If the department chair informs you that there is too much on the agenda to give you a few minutes, do not despair. Ask the chair if she would be willing to forward an e-mail to the faculty (and graduate students, if appropriate) with similar information. For large departments, this task may actually be handed off to an office assistant. Then you can craft a brief e-mail, welcoming folks back to school after summer (or winter holiday) break, and giving them similar information as you would if you were actually standing before them in the meeting. At some future time, you may want to create your own mailing lists for the entire history faculty, as well as targeted groups (e.g., the American specialists, women's studies faculty, students only, both graduate students and faculty, etc.) for special information or announcements. Most people get more e-mail than they want, so be considerate, and do not constantly barrage them with every minor update on a new resource, inane snippets, or information of questionable relevance. If you maintain a blog or use other social networking services, by all means direct their attention to your pages; just be aware than not all of the faculty will use those services, and even if they are behind the technological curve, you must serve them also through the means that best suits them (even if it means creating a printed newsletter and stuffing it in their department mailboxes—cut and paste makes this pretty easy).

Besides introducing yourself to the department chair and faculty, get to know the department's staff assistants. They can be very useful in getting important library announcements to faculty and students; sometimes assistants are even more effective than entrusting e-mails to the department head. These administrative assistants may also be able to put your name and e-mail information on the lists for open lectures and forums, department-wide announcements, and other useful information that will keep you informed of what is happening outside the library's walls.

Start Early with New Faculty

If your history department is fortunate enough to be hiring new faculty, get to know them as soon as you can when they arrive on campus. It may only be a short time before classes begin and they will have lots of questions regarding various library services such as course reserves, interlibrary loan, and bibliographic instruction. If your library produces a new faculty welcome kit, with contact e-mail addresses and phone numbers, descriptions of services, building hours, and location, be sure your faculty (especially the new ones) receive one. If your library does not make something like this, why not? It need not be complicated. Most of the material probably already exists on the library's website, but new faculty members may not have immediate computer access in their offices, or it may take several days before they are in the system to allow remote access. The faster they can get up and running with the library resources and services, the more they will appreciate it.

Engaging Professionally

Whether meeting history faculty in a departmental meeting or one-on-one, you should avoid empty flattery or gushing over your favorite history teacher in high school or college.

You are building a professional, working relationship, and you are representing your library to another department on campus. You want to make as good a first impression as possible. Recall how contemporary librarians generally cringe when some ingenuous person prattles, "Oh, you must *love* working in a library; being able to read all those books." First or even second meetings are not the time to mention that Stephen Ambrose is your favorite historian, or your sibling happens to be a member of the Society for Creative Anachronism or dresses up in Union blue or Confederate gray for Civil War reenactments on weekends. There are a number of professional historians who have little patience for amateur dilettantes playing dress-up, or even authors of best-selling histories marketed for a mass audience. On the other hand, most faculty in history (as well as other fields) are reasonable people. As you get to know members of the department better, you will learn with whom you can enjoy discussing the college football season (or lament, depending on the fortunes of your team), which member also participates in historical reenactment groups, and who is the prickly prima donna who believes, no matter how sterling the reputation of the institution where they happen to be, that they deserve to be somewhere better (this latter type can be found in every department on any campus). Remember, you are building relationships with people, and these do not happen overnight. Time and circumstance will be your allies.

During these initial meetings, it will be tempting to make all kinds of promises regarding library services and resources to appeal to the faculty or to make a better first impression. Resist this temptation at all costs; even during flush economic times, because you never want to promise more than you can deliver. Despite your best intentions, library or institutional priorities (or just plain inertia) will prevent you from achieving everything you might want to do in your first few months on the job. You might be surprised at how expensive some resources may be. Do not promise miracles, especially in open department meetings. It is extremely unprofessional and counter-productive at multiple levels to metaphorically write checks your library is unwilling or unable to cash, so be honest and realistic in your expectations and communications. During lean budgetary times, you may need to be more creative about fulfilling faculty requests for resources (or even recommend postponing the request), no matter how necessary or legitimate the request may be. If your library subscribes to JSTOR, it may be that the print versions of these titles need to be removed to a remote storage facility to create more shelf space for monographs. Think about what avenues are actually open to you before promising to bulldoze a new road (or purchase access to that great, new, primary source database). Remember, you can do everything right, and things may still not work out. Keep in mind that you may be one of several competing for scarce resources; the key is to not give up and to keep working the system.

Identifying Relevance

Be sure and learn the differences in needs and working styles among the faculty. You will want to offer a variety of information during your initial contacts or presentations to the faculty, but you also need to become an active listener. You need to listen carefully to what the faculty say they need. Sometimes they may describe a service that your library already provides, but under a different name or description based on experiences at other institutions. It is rewarding to provide instant gratification in letting them know the service is available locally after all. Other times you will pick up on resource needs they may not realize they wanted. Active listening also lets you tailor future interactions to be more relevant to each individual faculty member. Announcing a new medieval database to a twentieth-century military historian will not get the desired reaction that an announcement of the acquisition of an important set of microfilms on military training during the 1930s might. Think of Dr. Jones, your medieval specialist who spends his summers and research time in Great Britain as the vast majority of the esoteric primary sources he needs are overseas and may never be digitally available. Now consider Dr. Smythe, an American historian who spends her research time plowing through your library's exhaustive collection of New England prayer books for images of and references to women. Dr. Jones may be most concerned with the efficiency of the library's interlibrary loan service for needed secondary or reprint materials, whereas Dr. Smythe may already have a much closer working relationship with the special collections librarian and may bring her classes to the rare books room on a regular basis. Think about what you can offer to her and her students outside of the special collections department. Besides the treasures in rare books, her students will also need book reviews, scholarly journal articles, and books about their topics from the library's circulating collection. Even within the same history department, there will be very different research and teaching needs. Also, avoid looking at Dr. Smythe's relations with your special collections librarian as a competition. Rather, you are both on the same team, or partners, delivering needed services and resources to faculty and student members of the campus community.

It cannot be stated often enough that libraries are the laboratories for historians. They, and their students, spend a great deal of quality time within our buildings using our collections. This gives rise to several points of concern. Because they spend so much time in the library, some individual faculty members may develop the attitude that they already know all there is to know about your library and its resources, therefore they have no need to waste valuable classroom time bringing their students over for a library skills session for their research papers. Their students frequently show up at the reference desk in a confused state. These are often the same professors you will hear complaining at the end of the semester about the poor quality of research their students turned in. Actually, every department on campus has at least one of these characters. This individual will never be convinced of the value of bibliographic instruction no matter how many times it is offered. These are frequently the same faculty who will also express great surprise and delight at their recent discovery of a library database on their area of specialization; a database to which the library purchased access two years ago amid great fanfare. Do not despair; there are rarely more than one or two in a department. If you do a good job, other members of the department will recognize your value and in time sing your praises to such a degree that the supposedly experienced faculty user will come to value your knowledge as well.

Another point of concern is that some historians tend to assume or develop a sense of ownership over the portions of the collection they use most often. Visit a typical such professor in his office and you will see his shelves lined with library books on his research topic, even the one he finished seven years ago (how many are overdue and considered lost by the catalog, you would do well not to think about). His response to the news that certain titles are being selected for remote storage can range from panic, to indignation, to hostility, to checking out the entire seventy-volume set of the *War of the Rebellion: A Compilation of the Official Records of the Union and Confederate Armies* and hoarding it in his office. This is done despite the fact that this set is freely available and searchable electronically via the "Making of America" project at Cornell University. These professors may tell their students to bypass the online catalog and instead "go to the third floor, and use the books on the first three rows of shelves on your left for your papers." Working with these faculty members will take a great deal of patience, tact, and time spent looking for and promoting viable alternatives. One additional important caveat in working with faculty in any department outside the library: it is absolutely imperative that you avoid becoming entangled in departmental political battles. This may be easier said than done, especially as you try to establish a relationship with them. No matter which side tries to claim the moral high ground, you must remember to stay above the fray.

WHAT ARE THE LOCAL INSTITUTION'S NEEDS?

Faculty at any level of higher education will desire to have access to a wide range of materials to support their research and teaching roles; even the community college may be seen as a stepping-stone to a more research-oriented position. However, community colleges, smaller liberal arts schools that do not offer advanced degrees, and schools where the primary curricula center on science and technology may not have a strong institutional need for an extensive history collection. Frequently the library's priorities and budget will reflect this. Where faculty are rewarded primarily for teaching, there may be less demand for a deep collection of primary materials or a wide range of specialized journal titles. Conversely, even at these types of institutions, librarians should be aware that more of these faculty are incorporating some primary materials into lower-level undergraduate assignments as part of the outcomes-based education initiative and accreditation. Librarians assisting with these classes need to be aware of what the course assignments are and what library resources are available that will provide the best results. At small, highly selective liberal arts colleges, upperclassmen often must turn in a senior thesis or capstone research project in their major. For history majors, this is often a significant research paper of up to thirty pages, often based on primary source research. They will need access to the sources (interlibrary loan counts) and a knowledgeable librarian to help them. Meanwhile, at midsized universities with larger libraries that may be more likely to have dedicated subject specialist librarians, there will be increased needs for a wide variety of sources, either on-site or accessible electronically or via interlibrary loan. Faculty at these institutions may teach more classes than top-tier research universities, but may still be expected to maintain an active research agenda as part of the university's goals. They may ask for library instruction sessions specifically tailored to the topics covered in their classes. Similarly, at larger research institutions offering advanced degrees in history, the faculty may be under more pressure from the stereotypical publish-or-perish model. Faculty at these institutions are rewarded primarily for their research skills. Teaching is important, but does not carry the same weight as publications. Research faculty will need library support in the form of deep collections, as well as access to sources beyond the holdings of their local library.

A librarian for history should become familiar with the mission of the local institution as well as the individual department. As mentioned earlier, getting out of the library and visiting the faculty in their offices can be very helpful in discovering what types of library resources the faculty need most. In many instances, a personal visit from a librarian asking about what the faculty members do and offering the library support that they need will be a very pleasant surprise, particularly for the librarian to be actively listening and showing genuine interest in their responses! Most historians acknowledge their dependence on libraries and might welcome the opportunity to discuss issues with a librarian. Additionally, liaison librarians for any subject should make a point of learning the strengths and the research and teaching emphasis of the departments that they serve. Department websites often list such useful information as faculty names, contact information, and areas of research and teaching.

Supporting Tenure and Promotion

Librarians should familiarize themselves with the promotion and tenure requirements for history faculty at their institutions. Why should librarians (especially those not on the tenure track themselves) care about tenure requirements in other departments? The faculty, especially newly hired faculty on the tenure track, will care a great deal about tenure, and it is an integral part of academic librarianship to serve the research and teaching needs of the faculty. Tenure has often been erroneously called "a guaranteed job for life." All tenure really means is that the institution which granted a person tenure must follow its own established rules of due process in order to fire the tenured person. Tenure protects faculty members who research or teach topics to which members of the institution's administration or outside political organizations might have objections. It offers the freedom to follow lines of inquiry wherever they might lead. Tenure may be revoked for malfeasance involving state grant money or endangering students, but it cannot be revoked on a whim just because the current university president or governing board does not like a tenured professor's research findings.

Although students are important and a new crop comes in every year, faculty members (especially if they survive the tenure and promotion process) may be at your institution for the next thirty years, and you want to maintain a good working relationship over that time. Tenure requirements can vary widely according to the institution's overall mission and will affect nearly all services that librarians provide, ranging from information literacy programs to collection development policies and interlibrary loan services. Sometimes these tenure and promotion criteria can be found on a department's website. At smaller institutions, it may take more digging around. As you meet and develop relationships with faculty, it may be easier to just ask what their tenure requirements look like.

At many research institutions across the United States, a single-authored, scholarly monograph, preferably published by a highly respected university press, is a standard minimum requirement for tenure and promotion from assistant to associate professor rank. Often, this is an expanded or repackaged version of their dissertation. Because of the depth of research required to write such a book, faculty at research institutions will need to consult more monographs and journals, in addition to primary source materials. Depending on their topics, they may spend their summers looking for primary materials that cannot be acquired through interlibrary loan. They may need your assistance by identifying the archives they need to visit (some may even be on other continents) or navigating online finding guides to specific collections. The monographs these faculty produce are often rather esoteric and very narrowly focused, and they will be asking for access to library materials of a similar arcane nature. It is important for these young faculty to establish themselves as experts within their chosen field, capable of contributing original research to the profession, and thus their research will reflect this sometimes obscure focus. Access to the resources available to support their research can make the difference between career success or failure. As more and more primary materials become available in digital formats, faculty may call upon you, the history librarian, for assistance in navigating new interfaces or finding computer-based primary materials, or to teach these skills to their graduate students.

Research faculty in history, along with candidates for advanced degrees in history, must demonstrate an intimate familiarity with both the breadth and depth of the literature in their chosen field. Therefore their need for deep collections of scholarly monographs on a wide variety of topics is very great and they frequently must rely on interlibrary services in addition to trips to other repositories of sources. At smaller, less research-focused institutions, the standard for tenure may not be quite as high. As an alternative, at some smaller universities where the balance of research and teaching are more equitable, the standard may be a book published by a university press (with less concern for its rank) or a reputable commercial publishing company. Similarly, at other smaller universities, instead of a single-authored monograph, a combination of scholarly articles, book chapters, edited contributions, and book reviews may suffice.

Identifying Teaching Support Needs

Beyond the promotion and tenure requirements, librarians should also be familiar with the teaching needs of the local history department and the institution as a whole. Carefully examining the school's course catalog can be an important starting place because it lists the courses the department offers. Despite the dramatic shifts in research that the field of history witnessed in the past half century, many departments still teach a large number of undergraduate courses in the traditional manner of kings and presidents. There may also be regional subtleties and areas of emphasis as well. For example, the American Civil War is a perennially popular topic at institutions located in the southeastern United States. Labor issues could be popular in the more industrialized sections of the country, whereas agricultural labor and immigration issues are popular in the American Southwest. State and local historical topics find enthusiastic audiences everywhere. Additionally, it cannot be emphasized enough that getting out and talking with history faculty members about the courses they teach, the assignments they give, and their expectations of student work will be the most helpful means for subject specialist librarians to get to know the faculty and their needs. It also provides an opportunity for you to head off potential problems such as an assignment based on resources the library does not own or cannot access electronically. Community colleges may only offer a few basic courses in history and depending on the enrollment may not require much in the way of student research. These institutions will have less need for extensive monograph collections, a wide selection of journal titles, and deep primary documents resources. Librarians in these institutions will need to focus on finding materials that have more immediate appeal for the courses taught. Depending on the location of your institution, instructional sessions may be more directed to local resources in order to teach methodology and research skills, rather than focusing on a specific topic. Small liberal arts colleges may do little in the fields of advanced research, but in the more academically challenging institutions, junior- and senior-level students may be required to utilize primary sources in capstone term papers. Oftentimes, these teaching institutions may have smaller class sizes and thus may be open to more innovative information literacy skills programs. At research institutions offering graduate degrees in history, or even at smaller but highly competitive and academically challenging colleges, deeper collections and information literacy classes may be required. The history courses taught will cover a wider range of topics, the faculty expectations of student work as well as their own research will be higher, and the need for both a broader and deeper collection of library materials, especially primary source materials, will be greater (Arant and Mosley 2000; Kitchens 2001).

As mentioned earlier, perusing the history department Web page, the course catalog, class schedules, and descriptions of the institution can yield valuable information about how the library and library services are likely to be used. If, for example, a college does not have a scholar in Asian history, the collection in that area need not be extensive as few, if any, courses on that topic will be offered. On the other hand, if the institution has just hired a new faculty member whose specialty is feudal Japan, a collection may need to be built from scratch to support new courses and possibly graduate students. Problems can arise if the new faculty member was enticed by administrative promises regarding the library's ability to support their research and teaching with specialized materials (unfortunately this is not an unprecedented occurrence and resolution often takes a great deal of patience, diplomacy, and resolve within the library). Similarly, library staff may need to be given orientations to resources likely to be used for topics that semester, which will be encountered in reference transactions. At institutions with fewer faculty members, some may teach outside their primary area of expertise; however, even these do not generally stray too far afield. Note that not every course for which a description exists will be offered each semester. Also, there may be special topics courses that are not part of the regular curriculum, but appear on a semester-by-semester basis. Many times these are upper-level undergraduate courses, but select graduate courses are also often listed as such. Additionally, special topics courses with a historical focus need not be limited only to the history department, but may be cross-listed with other departments or taught by any department. A special topics course in sociology may examine the history of the discipline with particular emphasis given to nineteenth-century theorists Max Weber and Karl Marx. These special topics or capstone courses will frequently require students to use a mix of primary and secondary materials. If a new area of emphasis is defined and the library does not otherwise have extensive holdings in these areas, a librarian should try to acquire reference materials, indexes, databases, or other sources that at least provide bibliographic access to these resources so the students can request the materials through interlibrary loan. In addition to acquiring these materials, the class may also need instruction in how to efficiently use these materials, especially if the interface is unlike other common electronic reference sources.

Most often, assignments requiring primary sources are simply research papers in which the students must use a selection of both primary and secondary sources. The length of the paper and number of resources will vary according to class level, with higher-level classes requiring more than lower-level courses. However, in an effort to make even lower-level classes more engaging and interesting, some faculty may get creative with their assignments. As the history librarian, you may be called upon to teach library skills classes to these students, which are covered in more detail in chapter 5. While graduate students may be adept at using a library (or they may think they are), if they earned their earlier degrees from a different institution, or are older, non-traditional-aged students, they will need orientations or workshops to learn how to make the most of your library and the resources you have to offer. If your library has some unusual quirks, such as a significant portion of your collection that is classified and shelved by a different call number system, these students will need to be informed. One solution is to work with the history professor who is in charge of or directs the graduate program. Some departments have a department-run orientation day for new graduate students. You will find it productive to get on that calendar of events, and hold a session to introduce yourself and some of the most important features of the library (your online catalog, accessing online databases from off-campus, floor layout, service points such as reference, course reserves, circulation, and interlibrary loan), and a basic demonstration of your library's OPAC.

Teaching history can be seen as multidimensional. On one level, the instructor teaches what happened. These are the often dry facts that cause most students' eyes to glaze over. On a deeper level, instructors try to teach the students to think more critically and analytically about the past. This is one of the rationales behind using primary documents. Aside from the fact that examining resources perhaps created over a hundred years ago may hold a special thrill for some, requiring the students to examine an old document and think about what it says, what bias it may have, and what this says about the person or society that created it is at the heart of history instruction (Kitchens 2001).

Other Departmental Needs

Serve your clientele well and you may find yourself and your library used for recruiting. When departments hire new faculty members, tours of the campus are often part of the on-campus interview process. Since historians are so dependent upon the library for their work, it stands to reason that departments may want to show off their advantages regarding access to library materials, dedicated librarian resources, or other library services, especially if the department is competing against more prestigious institutions for a particular candidate. Since on-campus interviews rarely last more than two days and there will be a number of meetings with these faculty groups or that dean, and the candidate is expected to give a significant presentation on their research (and even, perhaps, lead a class either in lecture or readings discussion), the amount of time allotted to the library for a tour may be only thirty minutes to an hour. In some ways, it is not so very different from a fifty-minute instruction session, although usually with a single person it is easier to walk around the facility and show where the service points are. Sometimes, it can be beneficial or even enlightening to take the prospective faculty member up into the stacks to an area where she would find the majority of her resources. As she looks for particular titles significant to her work, you may be surprised at the gaps or the comprehensiveness of your collection. Depending on the nature of her research, you may want to organize a visit to your special collections library, but only if time permits and her research interests match a particular collection strength. Be mindful of the prospective faculty member's schedule, as making him late for his next appointment could have disastrous ramifications. Inclusion in the faculty recruitment process allows you to meet potential new faculty members and have an idea of where you should be planning in future collection needs. If your library's collections are not deep in that particular area, it also gives the prospective faculty member advance warning or even a negotiating tool for extra money for library enhancements from the department, college, or university administration.

Every so often, departments go through an accreditation process, and depending on how it is run, you as the history librarian may be asked to supply information about the library's collection for the report. Although the exact nature of this data will vary, it generally includes a volume count of the history books, number of journal titles, and perhaps number or titles of electronic resources. There may also be a request for the number of materials in foreign languages, since historians studying the history of other countries are expected to have a reading knowledge of the languages associated with their research. In order to accommodate these requests, you may have to consult with the person in charge of your integrated library system. The requests may be too complex for the public side, or even the technical side, of your library's OPAC. Hopefully, the department will contact you well in advance, so you have plenty of time to figure gathering this data into your normal workload. Unfortunately, it does not always work that way and you may be given only a couple of days or a weekend to provide the necessary data. Chocolate helps during this crisis, and beer or wine (in moderation, of course) are nice after the data is turned in. Be sure to share these with your systems librarian as this may be a recurring event several years later.

Working with the Local Community

In addition to the obvious patrons who are institutional faculty, staff, and students, there may be local, community users of a library's resources. Institutions that receive state or local financial support, institutions participating in the Federal Depository Library Program (FDLP), or even private institutions that happen to be the largest library of consequence in the area will have people from the local community using the collections. Genealogists, as they research their family history, will be especially interested in state and local historical resources. These could include old community maps, local business and professional directories, census records, as well as many other kinds of old county and city records. Some institutions may keep such material in their special collections area. Others keep only a very limited amount of this type of material available, if at all. Institutions in counties or cities that have large public libraries with a department dedicated to keeping state and local history records and materials may not require large local history collections. A public or private institution of higher education, whether it is considered a research institution or not, if it is the largest library in a wide geographic area, should maintain a respectable local history collection with as many local census records (and even local government and tax records) as possible. This is particularly important if the area once held an important place in history for economic, political, or military reasons. Maintaining these types of collections, as well as a collection on genealogical research materials, is another way of serving a legitimate population of interested users, and it builds goodwill with the community. For more information about genealogical materials, the History Section of RUSA has two committees and an e-mail list dedicated to genealogy and local history (see http://www.ala.org/rusa/sections/history/committees).

Some libraries may value librarians who conduct workshops for genealogists or give presentations to local history societies on topics of interest within the community. Local chapters of heritage groups such as the Daughters of the American Revolution or the Sons of Union Veterans of the Civil War or other historical reenactment groups may see the history librarian at the local college as an attractive meeting speaker to give a presentation on what resources they might be interested in for their programs or history research needs. These nonprofessional history researchers will frequently have a particular agenda and expectations of what they will find in the historical record. They are not under the same constraints of professional historians to be more objective and critical of the information. Heritage groups are generally more interested in celebrating their ancestors than facing historical reality. This might include reverifying family lore that claimed Great-Great-Great-Great-Great-Grandpa was a dashing, high-ranking cavalry officer. Unfortunately, reality may show he was a common foot soldier on the front line (or worse, either never saw action or was captured during his first skirmish). Members of these groups can develop some tunnel vision that nothing else matters beyond their particular ancestor; when, if they began to look a little more broadly at what their ancestor's neighbors had or did, they could create a more meaningful and more thorough family history. Unfortunately, attempting to show them the error of their ways (or at least, interpretations), no matter how delicately handled, can create a significant backlash, and you do not want your library's reputation to suffer for this. Sometimes, these people can be major donors, both in terms of materials or financial support. Tread carefully and discuss what resources the library has without making any value judgments. In these situations, bringing in a trained archivist, as a partner who may be accustomed to working with such groups, may be appropriate.

CONCLUSION

This chapter has been all about getting to know the historians you find yourself needing to serve. Establishing relationships takes time, but it need not be traumatic or difficult. For introverted librarians, it may take some creative thinking and becoming comfortable with their role as an academic professional. If personal meetings do not work, our modern communication-driven age offers several venues including e-mail, print, telephones, social networking sites, and news feeds; and who knows what will be available just a few years hence? The needs of history faculty and their students are very great and they have a vested interest in what happens in the library. Chemists have their laboratories with burners and beakers; astronomers have their telescopes and observatories; archaeologists have their field excavation sites; historians have the library. History librarians are admonished to listen carefully to their needs, both for teaching and research. Perhaps they want their students to be taught how to use their favorite database. Perhaps a faculty member wants the library to acquire a large collection of very esoteric materials they believe critical to their present research project. Perhaps the new crop of graduate students needs to be introduced to the basic library services at their new institution. These are just some of the ways librarians and libraries serve historians. In meeting these needs, the differences between a community college, small liberal arts college, private midsized university, or huge top-tier research university will only be matters of scope, scale, and comprehensiveness.

Even as one is building a relationship with the faculty, beware the pitfalls of departmental politics and the temptation to promise more than you can deliver. Each of these can lead to disaster, loss of credibility, and damage to bridges between the department and library that may take years to repair. Be conscientious; listen carefully and actively to what the concerns and needs of the faculty really are. Above all, be professional. Conduct yourself as the professional you are, respecting others and serving all to the best of your ability and within the limits of your library. Be patient serving those on the trailing edge of technology rather than the cutting edge; it may be less glamorous, but the service will be much appreciated and is needed. Finally, remember that not all people interested in historical research are limited solely to members and students in the history department. Faculty in other campus departments may be researching topics within their discipline that have a historical element. There are also members of the local community who may use your library for their own historical research, whether they are searching for lost ancestors, or to add that extra piece of realism to their costume for the upcoming historical reenactment event. Serving historical interests groups within the local community will help establish or maintain good relations with your institution.

4

REFERENCE SERVICES AND ACCESS TO MATERIAL

Like many other library patrons, when historians need assistance, the reference department is often a first stop. While every reference transaction is unique in its own way, historians (and their students) bring a specific set of needs that librarians and staff working a traditional or a virtual reference desk need to be aware of. Since not every class receives a library instruction session and you may not be to the point of assignment consultations with each faculty member, the reference service desk staff are often the first to learn about a particular assignment. This is especially true for interdisciplinary areas (such as a communications class studying political rhetoric from past presidential campaigns) when the history librarian is not necessarily involved ahead of time. Even though historians rely heavily on monographs and primary sources, there are several tools they use as access mechanisms for identifying supporting secondary resources. These include indexes and databases, published government data, reviews, and bibliographies. In distinguishing these from the types of materials used by historians and presented in other sections of the book, this chapter focuses primarily (but not exclusively) on resources that are typically given a "Reference Collection" designation. However, in our modern era of full-text searching of databases and e-books, the definition of "access" begins to blur as our patrons can search our reference tools remotely and follow the provided links to the actual text.

GET TO KNOW YOUR COLLECTION

While it would be too much to expect a librarian, especially one at a major research institution, to know from memory every book, every journal, and every database the library has, having a thorough familiarity with what types of resources you have, an awareness of major collected works, and a knowledge of many of the available databases of interest to historians makes your job as history librarian much easier. When the student contacts you with the inevitable topic of the RMS *Titanic* disaster and needs multiple primary sources for a sizeable research paper, you can quickly recommend looking at not only your library's subscription to Gale/Cengage Learning's the *Times* (London), but also suggest ProQuest's

New York Times (Historical) for the perspective of the intended destination of the doomed ship, and the reactions of the crowds and the survivors as they were brought in. Knowledge of your collection may tell you that your library does not have electronic access for the 1910s to H. W. Wilson's *Reader's Guide to Periodical Literature* (which in electronic format was known as *Reader's Guide Retrospective*; however, following a June 2011 buyout of H. W. Wilson by EBSCO, details on possible changes were not available at the time of this writing). Therefore you will have to show the student how to use the print to find a wealth of magazine articles on the tragedy and its aftermath. Despite many library users' expectations and desires that all necessary information be instantly accessible electronically on their computer screen, when it comes to information resources for historical research, we truly are living in a time of transition between print and electronic: some libraries simply cannot afford access to electronic versions of printed indices for the nineteenth and early twentieth centuries or to many of the electronic databases that reproduce primary sources. Also, many important materials have not yet been digitized either by for-profit companies such as ProQuest, Readex, and Gale/Cengage, or nonprofit research institutions such as the Library of Congress, University of Michigan, Cornell, Duke, University of North Carolina, and many others. In such cases, you must either find alternative sources that contain the same information, or the person you are helping must be willing to accept that full-text online may not be an option, and use the multistep process of finding a list of citations to prospective articles in the printed index, followed by searching for the titles among the library's resources.

It may seem trivial, but all librarians, especially new history librarians, should spend some quality time browsing the stacks of the circulating collection. You may be surprised by what you find (or do not find!). Again, having more than just a passing familiarity with the collection will help you be a better librarian. You do not have to know that your library's copies of the collected papers of George Washington are bound in green or brown covers (depending on the series) and shelved on the fourteenth row to the left as one gets off the elevator on the fourth floor. But it might not be a bad idea to know whether or not your library has that set. Similarly, knowing that your library does not have electronic access to *Hansard's Parliamentary Debates* will help if the faculty member for British history at your institution asks you about including assignments based on that resource on her syllabus next semester. Finally, when the student who has procrastinated all semester long finally gets around to working on his history paper, you can give him the mixed news that while some of the primary sources he needs can be accessed online through the library's subscription to the *Eighteenth Century Collection Online*, other useful material that would really help him get the grade he needs in this class are not available in your library. Since he no longer has time for interlibrary loan, assuming a library would even lend documents from the 1700s or be able to make scanned images of all the pages he needs, his only other option is driving to the next town to visit another research university that has the sources electronically, as well as in the original print. For research-centered assignments, knowing important holdings at nearby public or consortia institutions can be just as useful as knowing your own.

THE REFERENCE INTERVIEW

When assisting historians or their students, a thorough reference interview becomes of paramount importance. For those librarians who may find themselves thrust into the public sphere from behind the scenes in technical services because of budget cuts and hiring freezes, a reference interview is simply an inquiry-based discussion that the librarian has with the individual needing assistance. Whether in a virtual world or a traditional reference desk, you want to ask as many open-ended, content-specific questions as you can. The more information about their needs you can glean from them, the better your recommendation of a resource that will meet their needs will be (Katz 2002).

Perhaps the most important questions to ask a student needing reference assistance for an assignment with a historical component are, "Did your professor ask your class to use primary sources? If so, do you understand what these sources are?" Even if both questions are answered in the affirmative, students (especially underclassmen) often have only a very tenuous grasp on the concept of primary source material. Thus begins what can turn into a rather lengthy consultation. Although the student may want the experience to be "find-5-articles-fast-and-get-me-out-of-here," most history research is an exploratory activity and requires much more negotiation and thought. It is here that what seemed to be a simple reference question morphs into on-the-fly library instruction. Rather than tie up a computer at the reference desk, a better course of action may be to find another terminal in a quiet section of the reference area, an office, or even a wireless-enabled laptop at a library table.

Interaction Method Concerns

Despite the popularity of virtual reference services, this level of consultation can be very difficult to conduct via electronic media. Even over the telephone it is all but impossible to effectively explain to a student what she needs to see. Sometimes more details about the student's project or the library's resources can be included in e-mail, and chat is typically live so questions may be almost immediately clarified. Nonetheless, this level of service is most effectively done face-to-face where both librarian and student can see the same screen at the same time and no one has to wait while the other party tries to type a coherent response, even if both are fluent in abbreviated IM/chat slang. The following is an excerpt from a hypothetical chat session:

User: Hi. I'm looking for stuff on women doctors from 1750 to 1850.

Librarian: Hello, I'll be glad to help you. I do have a few questions about how you are defining your topic. How are you defining *doctor*? In this time period, medical roles open to women generally meant being a midwife.

User: I'm not sure. This is for Dr. French's Women in History class and she was talking about midwives. So I guess I mean midwives. Were there other medical roles for women in this time period?

Librarian: Not so many as today. So what kinds of sources has Dr. French asked you to use?

User: According to the assignment, I have to find at least five primary sources and five secondary sources.

Librarian: Good. Has Dr. French spoken to your class about what primary sources are?

User: I think she did, but I missed that class because I was sick. I did look at her notes online, but I'm not sure what she means by "at the time."

Librarian: "At the time" just means the document (or source) was originally created during the time period of your topic (in your case, between 1750 and 1850). We do have a couple of databases that could give you full-text images of books

	and other materials originally published during this period. Are you interested in a particular geographical region?
User:	I'm not sure. Would the United States or Europe be better?
Librarian:	Well, can you read languages other than English, such as French, German, or Spanish?
User:	I took Spanish in high school, but I don't remember much from it. I think I'd rather stick to things in English.
Librarian:	That's perfectly fine. By the way, what kind of assignment are you working on for Dr. French? Is this a class presentation, or a research paper? And when is it due?
User:	Well, right now, I just have to do an annotated list of references that is due this Friday. Then we have to write a research paper using the sources later in the semester.
Librarian:	OK, today is Wednesday, so we only have a couple of days. Let's begin with one of the library's databases called *Early American Imprints*. This database contains works on many different topics, printed in North America between 1639 and 1820, mostly in English. If you go to the library's homepage, click on the "Databases" tab, and type in that title, you should see the link.
User:	OK . . . I did that.
Librarian:	Good. Now there are several terms you can try searching under. You probably want to put some topics together to get a smaller group of results. These would include "women and physician" and "female and physician" and "midwife" or "midwifery."
User:	OK. I got twenty-four results with the first term.
Librarian:	You will need to look through these to see which ones would be most relevant as you are thinking about the topic for your paper. One that might be good is the title written by Alexander Hamilton titled "The Family Female Physician; or, A Treatise on the Management of Female Complaints, and of Children in Early Infancy" published in 1793.
User:	Wait, what is this saying? I thought you said this was in English.
Librarian:	Some of these books will be a little difficult to read because of the old style of printing. In the eighteenth century, a printed *s* looked very similar to a printed *f*. I have found that reading it out loud to yourself makes it easier to figure out.
User:	So is there a way to get a shorter list? How could something from Aristotle be useful to me? Wasn't he some Roman philosopher or something?
Librarian:	A shorter list? Not really. And Aristotle was Greek, by the way, but he was very influential on medical thinking in this time. Have you used the library catalog before to find books?
User:	Yes.
Librarian:	Well, that will be a way to find secondary sources, or books that look at an event after the event. If you still need more primary sources, you can look at the bibliography or list of references used by the author, but we may not

	have it here and you might have to do a request to get the book from another library.
User:	OK. Is there any way to find shorter articles about my topic that would be easier to read?
Librarian:	Possibly. Have you ever used a library database resource called "America: History and Life"?
User:	No.
Librarian:	OK. Let's go back to the library home page.

The session continued beyond this point.

In breaking down this chat session, some potential problems with virtual reference begin to surface. First, canned responses may not be relevant, given the amount of extra information this librarian needed to give the patron. These sessions will generally be much longer than usual and may cause problems with wait times if a library's virtual reference system is a popular service. Then there was the specificity of the topic, and the numerous possible search terms the patron might use to get results. When searching historical databases, you generally are limited to using terms common at the time, rather than using modern terminology. Synonyms and alternate spellings are frequently a requirement. Finally, many of the full-text databases have embedded windows while the image files themselves are quite large. This may cause problems for co-browsing systems.

Key Clarifying Questions

When a student arrives (either at a virtual reference desk or a physical one) needing assistance with primary sources, important follow-up questions include

- inquiries on the student's topic (including defining both chronological period and geographical location);
- the student's timeline (is the paper due tomorrow or next month?);
- the scope of the project (is this a two-page compare-and-contrast essay of two primary sources, or a much longer research paper requiring multiple primary sources?);
- what the class is and who the professor is (which can help define the research methodology expectations that will need to be used); and
- whether the historical material is the primary, fundamental, and core part of the assignment, or is being used to give a background perspective.

Depending on the answers to these questions, you can then begin to direct the student to the most appropriate resources, and if necessary, assist them in finding what they need. Similarly, do not be surprised if most of the time is taken up with trying to get the student to refine the topic. Many students come in with topics either too broad or too narrow for the assignment. A student may insist on doing a three-page research paper about World War II (apropos for late elementary school, but hardly college-level) or they want to spend five out of ten pages of a paper on the Third Crusade discussing the nuances of the siege tactics of King Richard I at Acre in 1191. In each of these cases, the student needs to do some rethinking and redefining of the topics. While we as librarians can help the students in this exercise, it is their paper and they have to make the final call. In some cases, a gentle suggestion they need to discuss their topic further with their professor may be best.

Patience and Determination Required

Whereas some science reference questions may be quickly resolved by consulting the most recent edition of a particular spectrum handbook or industry standard, and some social science questions may be answered by finding a few scholarly articles or current case studies, history questions often go deeper into resources and may require more of an explanation to the patron of why a particular source was employed. This is often because history librarians can only recommend a particular resource as an educated guess. There is no way for you to definitively know that documents found in the Gale/Cengage database, *The Making of the Modern World*, will absolutely meet the student's needs for primary sources on slavery on the island of Barbados. Yes, documents about slavery in Barbados can indeed be found there; however, only the student can make the final call of whether a given document suits the need, and only after carefully examining the sources. This is something many undergraduate students and even some new graduate students seem to have trouble understanding. While many role-playing scripts, videos, and library-professional literature often show a smiling patron leaving the reference desk with exactly what answered the question, history reference transactions do not always give that immediate sense of gratification. Given time to ponder the topic and dig deeper into other databases or print collections, both the librarian and the student may find additional sources that work for their assignment. Librarians should make note of the student's contact information for just such a purpose. Because each student brings her own focus, bias, and understanding to the project, each research project will be different with its own unique resource needs, even when you have just finished working with the fifth student asking for primary sources on the origins of the Revolutionary War. Historical inquiry, when done correctly, is not a simple game of trivia, but a deeper, nuanced exploration into the existing historical records.

Finding the Right Information

"Why can't we just search Google and be done with it?" the exasperated student asks.

"Did you try Google already?" the librarian responds.

"Well, yes, but it wasn't giving me what I wanted and I thought you could make it work better." Ah yes, Google, the ultimate search function capable of finding all things worth knowing by this shallow, technology-addicted age, or so certain grouches and curmudgeons would have us believe. The fact is that Google, Yahoo, and any number of other similar Internet searching tools can bring up a lot of hits, thousands of hits on any topic typed into the search box. Unfortunately, only some of these are relevant hits and some hits create serious pedagogical challenges. Some of the hits lead to phony websites run by scam artists trying to steal credit information by charging for what they claim will be the requested data. Other hits lead to websites run by cranks or political hacks with an axe to grind and the Internet gives them a worldwide forum through which to pour their venom. Other sites cloak themselves with the trappings of academic respectability and only after deep investigation do they reveal their false nature; one such is the website for the Institute for Historical Review (http://www.ihr.org), an organization that claims to be an educational research center, but challenges whether the Holocaust happened. Sifting the wheat from the chaff is a laborious process and students should be reminded that library resources are much more reliable and efficient in bringing usable results. Librarians can take advantage of this teachable moment, where a lesson in information literacy can be brought home with directly relevant examples. Keep in mind, however, that not everything a general Internet search dredges up is garbage; some libraries have posted on the Internet collection finding guides to selected archival holdings that can be extremely useful, and search engines can find these. Sometimes these finding guides can save an out-of-town trip (or lead to one if an important source is within driving range). Also, more and more digitized content is being included in institutional repositories and is found using search engine inquiries, which can lead to some real gems of primary source material being found that otherwise might have languished unused in a corner of the archives.

As mentioned in an earlier chapter, sometimes the resources available at a particular library cannot answer the questions being asked. What then? It depends on who is asking the questions, the timeline, and the person's abilities. Is the person seeking information about a particular topic (a student with a short deadline)? If so, he may be able to change his topic to one better suited for a library's available resources. If the person is a graduate student writing a dissertation or a faculty member writing a grant proposal, extra effort is required. Here is where connections with other history librarians at other institutions can help. Are the materials available via interlibrary loan and can the person wait for materials to arrive? If so, either the student or the researcher should start by checking WorldCat or the Center for Research Libraries in Chicago (if your library is a participating member). What if a student needs primary source material about Joseph Stalin's secret police operating in the 1930s? Do any such documents exist in the United States? Have any of them been translated into English (because often the student cannot speak or read Russian)? Can the student's professor help translate any documents found that come in through interlibrary loan? Are there alternative sources, perhaps by outside observers (such as spies working for the West), that have been translated and published in English? Has the fall of the Soviet Union allowed microfilming or scanning of old Soviet-era documents to take place? If so, are these available via interlibrary loan? Can the student rethink the topic, or at least the initial approach, to make use of what sources can be found? Sometimes librarians end up with more questions than answers; and creativity, patience, and tact must frequently be relied upon to deal with these situations.

Protecting Yourself

It should not be so, but in today's litigious society, there is an important issue that must be mentioned in context of a reference interview. It is stated elsewhere in this book that language changes over time, and reference librarians helping a patron research a topic with a historical focus must be cognizant of this fact. The issue is that some terms that need to be used in order to bring up meaningful records may be considered offensive by some modern readers from a racial or gender point of view. It may well be that the terms were considered offensive during the historical period as well but were still widely used in printed sources. While this in and of itself seems hardly worth mentioning, the warning is offered on the off chance that someone not involved with the reference transaction happens to notice what terms are appearing on the screen and becomes offended. Librarians have long had a professional interest in the privacy of our patrons and take seriously the freedom to read and research whatever topic is of interest. However, reference transactions that take place in a virtual environment, where transcripts are saved and reviewed by a third party as part of the librarian's evaluation process, can compromise this expectation of privacy. It may not even be racial epithets that are the problem; perhaps it is a patron at a religiously conservative institution wishing to research birth control and abortion in the early twentieth century. The best advice would be to have the discussion with reference administrators ahead of time. A privacy screen on public terminals may be all that is needed. While many institutional cultures will not have a problem with this issue, there are some that might. Raising awareness with reference administrators regarding patron privacy, academic freedom, and potentially offensive search terms or topics may prevent a considerable amount of embarrassment later on. No one wants to appear in *The Chronicle of Higher Education* because they were seen using offensive language on the publicly viewable terminals at the reference desk.

CATALOGS AND CATALOGING

If your institutional cataloging practices are sound, the local catalog should be the first place you look for information to support history research. The items in the local catalog are what are (or should be) available to history faculty and their students. If the sources needed are books, these will appear with the call number (and maybe even a link to a floor map of the library showing what call numbers are located where). In the case of journals or newspapers, while the catalog does not index these materials, it will show seekers whether a library has a subscription and what holdings for the local library happen to be. Even in this day of electronic full text, many faculty (and even students) like being able to take something physical with them as they leave. In this respect, the local catalog is a librarian's best first resource and ally. One may have additional local resources to check if the library chose not to put records of electronic resources into the catalog but arranged for them to be accessed through a separate website. However, since more and more vendors offer MARC records as part of the subscription, the process has gotten easier.

Searching Tips and Cautions

One particular advantage some OPAC interfaces have is the ability to limit returns by a range of publication dates. This helps historical researchers by allowing them to limit the number of hits to only those published between, for example, 1725 and 1780. Combining the date limit function with what otherwise might be a very broad search string can yield much more meaningful results. This trick can be especially useful when a library has loaded the cataloging metadata for an electronic database such as *Early English Books Online* (EEBO) into its automated catalog system. Again, depending on which system a library uses, there may be a hypertext link the researcher can click on to take them directly to the item in the other database. There is one caveat with this technique. Sometimes, microfilm sets of old records were given a publication date of when the film set was published (often in the 1960s or 1970s), but not the date that the particular item of interest in the collection was made (which may have been in the 1800s). While OPAC date limit functions can be a great help in finding historical resources, they must be used with some caution.

Despite the advantages of local catalogs, when searching OPACs for materials on historical topics, there are some pitfalls that can create confusion for anyone, even seasoned desk staff. Much of the confusion arises out of certain cataloging practices. Issues develop because when an item is cataloged, there is no way for the cataloger to know all the ways it may be used. For example, "Primary Sources" is not a phrase that will be found in a Library of Congress Subject Heading (LCSH), much to the consternation of students and nonhistory librarians and staff. The controlled-vocabulary searching in most OPAC systems can be both an advantage and a disadvantage. While LCSH terms may seem quite stilted for many nonlibrarian searchers, skilled librarians can use them effectively to narrow the search to a more manageable and meaningful set of results, if they know what terms to include. Often, catalogers will use the word "Sources" in an LCSH field to indicate a work is a collection of documents, letters, diary, or other material that for some would count as excellent primary source material. Depending on the particular interface and system a library uses, reference librarians can force the search to include the term "Sources" in an LCSH to bring up this type of material.

Novice searchers are often frustrated by the semantic gymnastics of subject headings. For example, there is no LCSH for "World War 1," "World War I," or "First World War." There is, however, the LCSH for "World War, 1914–1918." Sometimes folks are confused when they see the LCSH "World War, 1939–1945" because the bombing of Pearl Harbor, which precipitated U.S. entry into the conflict, happened in 1941. The designation covers the actual beginning of the hostilities in September 1939, when Germany invaded Poland. The United States did not become formally involved until two years later, a fact of which many American students may not be aware. Along a similar vein, the American Civil War of 1861–1865 is not the only civil war mentioned in an LCSH. In the seventeenth century, England fought a civil war; Spain had a civil war in the twentieth century; and there have been numerous other internal conflicts on almost every continent to carry that term. Awareness of terminology is therefore important; paying attention to the LCSH portion of a record that the patron indicates looks especially useful is also important; both can help when you are having trouble grasping what the patron is saying he needs. Sometimes it helps to execute a keyword search on a specific part of an LCSH. Combined with publication date limiters, this can return useful information.

Impact of Cataloging Practices

Another issue with catalogs that can frustrate historians, their students, and the reference librarians trying to assist them is the practice of minimal cataloging. Historians, like other humanities scholars, often need edition-specific information such as charts, maps, illustrations, and similar types of added material. This important information sometimes does not appear on a catalog record page, even if one selects a more detailed view. This lack of detail is particularly an issue with records purchased from book vendors. A source of greater frustration, however, is the practice of only attaching one or two overly generalized terms in the LCSH field. A case in point is eminent historian Natalie Zemon Davis's book of collected essays, *Society and Culture in Early Modern France*. According to WorldCat, there are four headings in the subject fields. Two of the headings are in English and the only differences between those two are an American spelling versus a British spelling, and the British version adds the term "Collections." The American heading is "France—Civilization." This single, very general subject heading does woefully little to help a reader decide if this book by a distinguished historian might serve her needs or not. Since subject headings are often hypertext links in modern catalogs, having more subject links from which to choose is a real boon for researchers and the librarians trying to assist them. If you have the opportunity to give feedback on cataloging practices at your library, encourage more detailed cataloging records for history-related materials (Kitchens et al. 2002; Hickey and Arlen 2002).

THE REFERENCE COLLECTION

The influence that you, as history librarian, have over a reference collection may vary from library to library. Since subject librarians are often asked to make recommendations or render professional opinions regarding reference sources, some of the issues surrounding this class of sources need to be addressed. Reference materials can include, but should not be limited to: catalogs, chronologies, indexes, encyclopedias, dictionaries, and bibliographies. These materials can be general in nature, or extremely esoteric and deeply detailed. Reference materials can also be in multiple formats, generally print and/or electronic. As previously mentioned, these sources can have any call number, as many "history of field X" works get shelved in reference collections. The amount of material a selector wants to put in a reference collection (or has physical space for) will vary widely and should be carefully considered. A small library without a large circulating collection and few journal titles may actually want to construct a large collection of print and electronic reference materials as a means of at least providing access and bibliographic citation information to its patrons in order to more easily facilitate finding and borrowing the desired items through interlibrary loan. On the other hand, if space is limited, librarians will need to be more selective when choosing printed reference resources and acquire electronic versions where available. Many publishers are converting a significant number of reference titles to electronic format, which can make these important resources easier to use (particularly in a virtual reference environment). Research libraries should have a reference collection that provides as much access to its local holdings and to national-level collections in as many ways as possible (East 2010; Katz 2002).

MAJOR INDEXES: ACCESSING SECONDARY MATERIALS ELECTRONICALLY

Indexes and databases are important reference sources for historians because they provide access to the scholarly, secondary literature. While many of the indexes to the secondary scholarly periodical literature do not provide full text for every article, links to aggregators or articles within e-journals are becoming more and more common. Examples of history-specific reference materials include the indexes to the secondary, scholarly journal literature: *America: History and Life* and *Historical Abstracts*. These two renowned resources were originally published by ABC-Clio. However, in 2008, EBSCO purchased these titles and migrated them to the *Academic Search* platform. Regardless of interface, these two titles are the most important indexes to the scholarly journal literature for the field of history. Despite being published by the same company and using a common interface, there are distinct differences that preclude one from substituting for the other. *America: History and Life* indexes scholarly articles from about two thousand journals from all over the world on topics relating to North American (U.S. and Canadian) history. The topics range from the most recent political scandals to ancient arrowheads left by prehistoric nomads in the Great Plains. *Historical Abstracts* indexes many of the same journals, but for topics relating to everywhere in the world *except* North America with subjects only going back to around 1450. Both titles began indexing journals in the early 1960s. Another significant difference between the two, despite their common origins, is that *America: History and Life* includes citations to book reviews while *Historical Abstracts* does not. Therefore, a historian looking for a review of a book on German history will need to search elsewhere (H. W. Wilson's *Book Review Digest* would be a good place to start, followed by JSTOR if the book is more than five years old). There are additional indexes that would appeal to historians in particular specialties listed. Some are obviously focused toward a historian's need. Others include "history of" a given area and add value from the historic depth of coverage. Many of these are available either in print or electronic format.

- EBSCO (as of 2011) *America: History and Life* and *Historical Abstracts* (http://www. ebscohost.com).

- H. W. Wilson Indexes (including *Applied Science and Technology Index, Humanities Index, Social Sciences Index,* and *Reader's Guide to Periodical Literature,* as well as "Retrospective" versions of each).. *Note*: In June 2011, EBSCO and H. W. Wilson merged, and Wilson resources have moved to the EBSCO interface.

- Paratext *19th Century Masterfile* (http://www.paratext.com).

- Brepolis *International Medieval Bibliography* (*IMB*) (http://www.brepolis.net).

- ISI (Thomson Reuters) *Arts and Humanities Citation Index* and *Social Sciences Citation Index* (http://www.isiwebofknowledge.com).

- ProQuest/CSA *Index Islamicus* and *Public Affairs Information Service* (*PAIS*) (http://www.csa.com).

- K. G. Saur Verlag *Internationale Bibliographie der Zeitschriftenliteratur* (http://www.saur.de).

- UC Regents *Hispanic American Periodicals Index* (*HAPI*) (http://hapi.ucla.edu).

- EI Village *Engineering Index* (http://www.engineeringvillage2.com).

A special type of indexing resources are those retrospective sources that provide bibliographic control for literature published in earlier times. These can be a boon for finding precious primary source materials. William Frederick Poole began publishing his index to the popular periodical literature of the day in the early 1850s. His project expanded to provide bibliographic access to many popular periodicals for much of the nineteenth century. Paratext now offers an online version of Poole's index as part of its *19th Century Masterfile*. Early in the twentieth century, the H. W. Wilson Company began publishing their well-known *Readers' Guide to Periodical Literature,* which carried on Poole's idea of a single index to provide access to a large number of popular periodicals across a wide variety of subjects. These indexes, as well as other indexes to newspapers and professional journals that began in previous centuries, can be a treasure trove for historians for whom these articles from the past represent the types of primary sources required by serious scholarship. H. W. Wilson has made most of its periodical indexes available online including many of the retrospective works, and although material older than the early 1980s is not yet available in full text, it remains to be seen how EBSCO will treat these records. There are also indexes to newspapers that function similarly. A printed index to the *New York Times* or the *Times* (London) has been available going back to the earliest days of each paper's publication, and newspapers can be a gold mine of primary source data for certain historical topics. Selectors should be cognizant that people engaged in historical research must have access to these indexes either in print or electronically. Therefore, you should use any influence you have to keep the printed version available in a reference area, or to recommend adding the electronic subscription to the older retrospective material.

OTHER TYPES OF INFORMATION

For many historians, even those not working in political or diplomatic fields, government publications are vitally important resources. Governments publish on any number of subjects and with the changes in the way history is written, many government materials are being used in different ways years after the publication date. Whereas previous generations of historians may have limited themselves primarily to official records of legislative bodies (Parliament, Congress, or state legislatures), current generations of historians add court opinions, census data, agricultural reports and publications, military reports, labor publications and reports, maps and drawings, engineering and other technical reports, taxation records, and statistics, just to name a few. The Internet provides many governments with an inexpensive method of publishing various kinds of information, but not all titles will be released in electronic format. Unfortunately for historians, most of the information published electronically by governments tends to be current information only. Historical data is often low on the list of digitization priorities, though some commercial databases providers are including historical government materials in their offerings. Historical government materials can be purchased through commercial companies such as Readex or LexisNexis (although as of 2010, LexisNexis sold much of its historical congressional material to ProQuest). Additional resources for government information include

- Government Printing Office Federal Digital System (United States) (http://www.gpo. gov/fdsys)
- Legislation.gov.uk (British legislation since 1267 by Her Majesty's Stationary Office) (http://www.legislation.gov.uk)
- Readex (publishers of the US Serial Set—early American government materials) ((http:// www.readex.com/readex))
- CIS (Congressional Information Service, formerly a subsidiary of LexisNexis; published an electronic version of the US Serial Set; LexisNexis recently sold numerous historical collections of congressional material to ProQuest) (http://cisupa.proquest.com/ws_ display.asp?filter=U.S. Serial Set Digital Overview)
- ProQuest/CSA *Public Affairs Information Service* (*PAIS*) ((http://www.csa.com))
- Cambridge University Press, *Historical Statistics of the United States* (Millennial Online Edition) ((http://hsus.cambridge.org))
- ProQuest *Ancestry Library Edition* and *HeritageQuest Online* (for census and other materials) (http://www.proquest.com)

Participant libraries in the United States Federal Depository Library Program (FDLP) have special issues to consider that affect library collections and use. The U.S. government has been using the Internet to publish many more titles than in the past. Many of these titles may only be available in electronic format. Conversely, some print titles have been withdrawn and repository libraries have been obligated to surrender their copies. The reasons vary, but include privacy concerns and identity theft on records that include personal identification information (e.g., Social Security numbers for a named and living individual) as well as national security reasons in this security-sensitive, post-9/11 world. For more information about the FDLP, go to the URL http://www.fdlp.gov.

ARCHIVAL MATERIALS

Prior chapters discussed the importance of primary source materials in historical research. Many of these materials can be found in special collections and archives around the world. As the history selector for the main collection, you may or may not have any influence over special collections or rare acquisitions; it is nevertheless an important part of reference services to provide access to tools for locating archival materials. Many academic historians spend their summers traveling to libraries or museums housing these rare but essential sources.

One of the earliest means of providing access to archival materials was the *National Union Catalog of Manuscript Collections*. Although published by the Library of Congress, it contained entries for materials held at institutions all over the United States. The print version of this resource has not been updated since 1993. However, there are now electronic versions of this resource and other means of providing access to manuscripts that history librarians can use to direct history researchers to the primary materials they need. In addition to the resources listed below, selectors should be aware that the Google search engine will find often selected materials listed in institutional repositories. Likewise, some special collections libraries have made their holdings findable through Google or other Internet search mechanisms. Others have cooperated to create homemade databases or purchased commercial products that allow distant users to search for collections and even finding guides (some down to the folder level!). Some repositories may have the facilities to scan selected documents and e-mail the files to distant patrons. However, because electronic delivery is only one of the issues (copyright and ownership are also important considerations), you should not assume this to be the norm. Selectors will most likely need to be aware of these commercial and noncommercial resources:

- Library of Congress, *National Union Catalog of Manuscript Collections* (http://www.loc. gov/coll/nucmc)
- ProQuest, *Archive Finder* (http://archives.chadwyck.com)
- OCLC, WorldCat (http://www.oclc.org/worldcat)

In addition to these sources, there may also be catalogs built and maintained by libraries at the state level or some other regional division.

PRINTED GUIDES, BIBLIOGRAPHIES, ENCYCLOPEDIAS, LANDMARK WORKS

For a historian, a bibliography is an especially useful tool as it provides a map back to sources that are closer to the original representation of the event or condition. Though not as common today as just a few years ago, printed bibliographies are still viable tools for historians. In all likelihood it will not be possible or even appropriate to house all bibliographies in the reference collection. However, there are some seminal works that are good reference tools because of their scope of coverage or level of authority. In 1995, the AHA published the third edition of *The American Historical Association's Guide to Historical Literature*. These two volumes contain 27,000 annotated titles of what a distinguished committee of editors considered to be some of the definitive works in history with a worldwide scope on a myriad of different topics. This work has geographical and chronological subdivisions and history selectors can pick and choose according to their needs. Some titles will no longer be in print and history selector librarians wanting to acquire these titles should consult both with history faculty and out-of-print book dealers to check need and availability (East 2010).

Another company, ABC-Clio, publishes excellent reference works including specialized encyclopedias such as the award-winning *African-Americans at War: An Encyclopedia* and

Southeast Asia: A Historical Encyclopedia from Ankor Wat to East Timor. Many of the ABC-Clio titles are available either in print or as electronic books, which increases their utility and appeal. Also, Fitzroy Dearborn Publishers (now Routledge) offers an excellent *Reader's Guide to . . . History* series that has an encyclopedic arrangement of subjects with a reading list of seminal works and a brief essay on each topic. In addition to the above-mentioned titles, librarians may wish to consult the following list of select titles as needed for their collection focus (some of which may be now available electronically):

Beisner, Robert L., and Kurt W. Hanson. *American Foreign Relations since 1600: A Guide to the Literature*. 2nd ed. Santa Barbara, CA: ABC-Clio and the Society for Historians of American Foreign Relations, 2003.

Black, Jeremy. *War in European History, 1494–1660*. Washington, DC: Potomac Books, 2006.

Eldevik, John. *Medieval Germany: Research and Resources*. Washington, DC: German Historical Institute, 2006.

Freidel, Frank. *Harvard Guide to American History*. Rev. ed. Cambridge, MA: Belknap Press of Harvard University Press, 1974.

Fritze, Ronald H. *Reference Sources in History: An Introductory Guide*. Santa Barbara, CA: ABC-Clio, 2004.

Glasrud, Bruce A., and Arnoldo De Leon. *Bibliophiling Tejano Scholarship: Secondary Sources on Hispanic Texans*. Alpine, TX: Sul Ross State University, Center for Big Bend Studies, 2003.

Hacker, Barton C. *World Military History Annotated Bibliography: Premodern and Nonwestern Military Institutions (Works Published before 1967)*. Leiden: Brill, 2005.

Lagorio, Valerie Marie. *14th Century English Mystics: A Comprehensive Annotated Bibliography*. New York: Garland Publishers, 1981.

Lincove, David A. *Reconstruction in the United States: An Annotated Bibliography*. Westport, CT: Greenwood Press, 2000.

Mathews, Robert A., ed. *French Revolution: Overview and Bibliography*. Hauppauge, NY: Nova Science Publishers, 2002.

Miller, Joseph C. *Slavery and Slaving in World History*. Armonk, NY: M. E. Sharpe, 1999.

McDevitt, Theresa. *Women and the American Civil War: An Annotated Bibliography*. Westport, CT: Praeger, 2003.

Perrault, Anna H., and Ron Blazek. *United States History: A Multicultural, Interdisciplinary Guide to Information Sources*. 2nd ed. Westport, CT: Libraries Unlimited, 2003.

Propas, Sharon W. *Victorian Studies: A Research Guide*. High Wycombe, UK: Rivendale Press, 2006.

Tompson, Richard S. *Great Britain: A Reference Guide from the Renaissance to the Present*. New York: Facts on File, 2003.

Wantanabe-O'Kelly, Helen. *Festivals and Ceremonies: A Bibliography of Works Relating to Court, Civic, and Religious Festivals in Europe, 1500–1800*. London: Mansell, 2000.

There are other materials appropriate to the reference collection that will be needed by historians. These resources will provide a novice historian, often a student but sometimes a senior researcher exploring a new perspective to their work, an overview of a topic and a bibliography to get her started digging for more. These resources may be single-volume handbooks or multivolume sets. Both Scarecrow Press and Greenwood Publishing offer a number of "Historical Dictionary of . . ."-type titles. Scarecrow tends to focus more on the history of individual nations or significant political entities (e.g., large cities), while Greenwood uses a topical approach, ranging widely from contemporary U.S.-Latin American relations to the Peace of Westphalia (the treaty ending the Thirty Years' War in 1648). Some additional examples of these are

Browne, Ray B., and Pat Browne, eds. *The Guide to United States Popular Culture*. Bowling Green, OH: Bowling Green University Press, 2001.

Fierro, Alfred. *Historical Dictionary of Paris*. Trans. Jon Woronoff. Lanham, MD: Scarecrow Press, 1998.

Lamar, Howard R., ed. *The New Encyclopedia of the American West*. New Haven, CT: Yale University Press, 1998.

Tenenbaum, Barbara A., ed. *Encyclopedia of Latin American History and Culture*. New York: Charles Scribner's Sons, 1996.

Vincent, C. Paul. *A Historical Dictionary of Germany's Weimar Republic, 1918–1933*. Westport, CT: Greenwood Press, 1997.

Weir, Robert E. *Class in America: An Encyclopedia*. Westport, CT: Greenwood Press, 2007.

Zeleza, Paul Tiyambe, and Dickson Eyoh, eds. *Encyclopedia of Twentieth-Century African History*. London: Routledge, 2003.

Finally, there are landmark works of historical research support that belong in every library, often in the reference collection. These titles have stood the test of time and/or are considered by scholars to be vitally important to teaching and research. The editors, publishers, and contributors have all earned the respect of their peers for work of outstanding quality. These titles include encyclopedias, guides, and bibliographies. The information contained may not be available elsewhere or in as neat and concise manner. Both Oxford and Cambridge University Presses offer series titles in this category, such as *The Oxford History of the British Empire* or *The Cambridge History of Russia*. Topics vary widely from eighteenth-century political thought to the Roman Empire. Some of the titles already mentioned in this chapter fall in this category, such as *The American Historical Association's Guide to Historical Literature* or the Fitzroy Dearborn Publishers' (Routledge) *Reader's Guide to . . . History* series. Other titles include the following:

Bentley, Michael. *Companion to Historiography*. London: Routledge, 1997.

Boyd, Kelly, ed. *Encyclopedia of Historians & Historical Writing*. London: Fitzroy Dearborn Publishers, 1999.

Garraty, John A., and Mark C. Carnes, eds. *American National Biography*. New York: Oxford University Press, 1999.

Gibb, H. A. R., J. H. Kramers, E. Levi-Provincal, and J. Schacht, eds. *The Encyclopedia of Islam*. New ed. Leiden: E. J. Brill, 1986. (Online access available.)

Matthew, H. C. G. and Brian Harrison, eds. *Oxford Dictionary of National Biography*. Oxford: Oxford University Press, 2004. (Online access also available.)

Roth, Cecil, and Geoffrey Wigoder, eds. *Encyclopedia Judaica*. Jerusalem: Keter Publishing and Macmillan Company, 1972.

REFERENCE ON LOCATION

These days it goes without saying that reference service can happen anywhere, anytime. Depending on the size of your community, if someone recognizes you as a librarian, they may feel free to ask you for assistance. When you are at the grocery store or placing an order at the local deli, people generally understand you do not have access to all of your resources, and may just be looking for a few good resources rather than a comprehensive list, or whether the building is open later that weekend. On the other hand, wireless computing and campus networks allow librarians to move out into their clients' spaces and bring more personalized services into departments or computer labs all over campus. Sometimes this is called "embedded librarianship" (Jacobs 2010) and it can be very useful. There is an interest in going to where the students are studying, such as coffee shops or student centers. Some administrative coordination may be needed in order to avoid sending too many librarians out to too many of the local coffee shops at the same time. Depending on one's tolerance levels, decaf is recommended for late afternoon hours if one hopes to sleep that night.

Established Office Hours

Just as teaching faculty keep established office hours for students to come by and receive assistance, you may also want to add set office hours to be held both inside and outside of the library building, specifically in your assigned academic department. If the history department has a computer lab for its own graduate students, it can be an excellent place for a librarian to offer reference assistance at a given time each week. If no dedicated lab is available, perhaps the librarian could hold court in the lobby of the history department's building with a wireless laptop and card table. This may be far from glamorous, but it can be effective. Although many might consider new freshmen to be the most needy of library users, this is not always the case for history students. Graduate students often need the most assistance since a higher level of research is expected of them, but they may not yet have developed familiarity with your library in the first semester or two. If their undergraduate work was done at a different institution, they may still be trying to learn the subtleties and processes (and even floor plan) of your library. Being available for consultation and basic reference in their setting can benefit both the students as well as the librarian. The students get personalized service from their subject specialist librarian. The librarian gets to know their clientele much better on personal levels, but more importantly regarding their plans for thesis and dissertation topics. For example, if a graduate student expresses interest in researching a particular topic, say a group of naval exercises in the 1920s, it may well be worth trying to purchase the microfilmed reports from those exercises if resources are available, rather than requiring the student to request them repeatedly from interlibrary loan every other month or so.

Reference On the Fly

Correlated to the idea of performing reference services outside of the library building is that which incidentally occurs while walking down the halls of the history department. When planning to visit one faculty member in their office, try looking up a second as well. Pay attention to what faculty are doing, and do not interrupt important business. Some faculty stay away from their office except when they absolutely must be there for established office hours and between classes to avoid interruptions in their research and writing. You may need to engage with these folks via e-mail. Other faculty are frequently in their office, reading in preparation for class, creating a visual presentation to accompany their lecture, writing the next chapter of their book, or some similar task. If they are meeting with students, try again later. On the other hand, often the response to your appearance will be, "Hi! I was just about to call (or e-mail or text) you. I need your help with . . ." They may need help navigating the library's home page, or a refresher on searching a particular database. Take this golden opportunity to observe carefully how they use the library's website and resources! You may be able to show them a more efficient method of finding the desired resource. You may also take back some ideas on how to improve the library's website or other interface issues. While assisting the faculty member, there will be opportunities to show new resources or services (or remind them of existing resources and services). Visiting faculty and students where they spend a considerable amount of their day (in their department) is a fruitful way to build relationships that can yield untold benefits for all down the road.

24/7 REFERENCE (OR CLOSE TO IT)

With some library buildings extending their hours to be open 24/7 for study, and a certain universal propensity among students to be working on research papers in the wee hours of the morning when trained library assistance is least available, you can address some of this need through annotated Web pages with links to important databases and other electronic resources. While these pages (often called "guides") are no substitute for assistance from well-trained staff or professional librarians, it is a place the students can go to at least get them started on their research until they can get in contact with the librarian for a more in-depth consultation regarding their specific needs. These subject guides should offer a wide range of available sources with brief explanations of the types of information that can be found with a given title. Again, the goal is not to answer every possible need, or list every single resource that could possibly be used, but instead to provide an authoritative list of resources that will get the person started until a more thorough consultation can be arranged. A sample subject guide might include the following information:

- Name and contact information for the history librarian.
- A reminder or definition of what primary sources are.
- A link to the library's catalog.
- A list of the most important indices and databases for scholarly, secondary material (e.g., *America: History and Life/Historical Abstracts*; JSTOR; Project MUSE; *Book Review Digest*; etc.). This list should be annotated to allow patrons to make informed decisions on which resource may best fit their needs.
- A list of databases and electronic resources for primary source material (annotated as the list for indices).
- A list of hypertext links to free resources for historical information (e.g., *American Memory, Making of America, Documenting the American South*, etc.) with annotations.
- A list of links to local and state historical materials.
- A list of links to professional organizations.

This list represents a minimum for a useful Web guide. Librarians are encouraged to use their own creativity and ingenuity to add images, sites, or links they believe will best suit their needs, and the needs of their clientele. Keep in mind that not all users are as tech-savvy as you might imagine, and while it is tempting to create a plethora of Web guides, having one or two broad guides to cover the vast majority of needs merits consideration.

Class Guide Caveats

Depending on local library requirements and how courses are taught, you may need to make subpages or separate Web pages for individual classes, depending on the preferences of the teaching professor. Some instructors may see this as a great help to their students; others may have educational objectives for having students do particular assignments in specific ways, or using a specified methodology. Once the assignment has been given, it is not your place to question the professor's technique or objective. If the professor chooses to include you in planning the assignments, all the better, but if not, stay out. More of this will be discussed in chapter 5, but if a professor gives the students an assignment that cannot be successfully completed with existing library resources, you should contact the professor as soon as possible and discuss alternatives. On the other hand, if a professor wants students to use specific, available resources, and did not request library assistance, and does not return your calls or e-mails, assume there is an educational objective to be accomplished and let it go. You may want to contact the professor after the semester about alternative resources, and offer a library instruction session, but do not force the issue if the professor declines.

Another issue regarding class-specific Web pages is overlap. Within a single history class the students may choose such a wide range of topics, there may be little need to create a class guide for that individual class if all it does is duplicate 75 percent of an existing subject guide. Even upper division courses, which can have a very narrow focus, may still have creative students wanting to explore such a variety of topics that ostensibly most of the resources currently listed on an overall history subject guide would be repeated on the class guide. Some professors may be delighted to have such a specific guide created for their class. However, keep in mind that sometimes class numbers and section numbers may change from one semester to the next. Also, particularly in classes below senior-level, a different faculty member may be teaching that course the next semester with a completely different approach and assignments. For example: one semester the class on nineteenth century Europe is taught by a faculty member whose specialty is the Chartists' Revolt in Great Britain in the 1830s, while the next semester that the course is offered, a specialist in the Franco-Prussian War of 1870–1871 is the instructor. There is nothing that mandates these professors must use the same texts or assignments. Depending on the institution, even within the basic 100-level survey courses, instructors may have a great deal of autonomy regarding readings, assignments, and whether to have a library research component, or not. Supportive Web pages need to reflect this aspect of academic freedom.

CONCLUSION

Reference materials and services are vitally important to people involved in historical research, whether professional historian, student, or amateur. When they arrive at a reference service point, whether that happens to be at a physical or a virtual reference desk, there are some special considerations that you must remember as history librarian. If the patron needs primary source materials, finding them among a given library's myriad print and electronic resources can be a challenge. Having more than just a passing familiarity with their subject collections will give you an advantage in providing efficient and helpful service. Conducting a thorough reference interview to ascertain the topic being investigated and the types of resources needed is another important factor to providing good service. Being proficient in searching the local automated catalog by knowing what terms are most effective or how to limit results to a more meaningful and manageable list is also important for librarians. Having a high-quality collection of reference materials can be particularly useful to researchers. Even small libraries with limited means or few electronic full-text offerings can expand their holdings far beyond their walls via interlibrary loan, but in order to most effectively use this service, sufficient bibliographic information must be provided. This is where indexes, bibliographies, and other reference materials are most useful. Not only can reference materials provide access to articles from journals not owned, but some can even open up the world of special collections and manuscript materials.

Reference service no longer happens just at a reference desk. Web pages dedicated to recommending sources for historical research with annotations will allow anyone doing any kind of historical research to pick and choose which resources best suit their needs, at least until they are able to consult with a librarian. Sometimes these types of pages can be made for individual classes, but given the wide range of topics, if a subject guide already exists, a class guide would frequently be redundant. Also beyond the traditional reference desk is moving into the departments. Advances in telecommunications and wireless computing allow a librarian with a wireless laptop computer to set up shop in a building lobby or office and establish dedicated office hours to assist students and faculty with their research or other library needs. This level of personalized service can be extended when librarians get out of the library offices to meet the history faculty in their own departmental offices. These meetings (which do not always have to be arranged ahead of time) offer opportunities to promote new or existing resources and services. It also gives you the opportunity to watch your clients work, which in turn can help you identify resources and services that best meet your clients' needs.

5
___

INFORMATION LITERACY FOR HISTORIANS

In a recent article appearing in *American Libraries*, Char Booth succinctly stated "Librarians are educators by default" (Booth 2010). She noted that anything from the most basic reference interaction to in-depth consulting, from creating an information literacy program for students to a comprehensive staff-training program, at its most basic element involves the librarian educating some other person. And she is absolutely on target. As professional librarians, we teach people how to find, assess, and use library and information resources. For librarians working in an academic setting, the idea of "librarian as educator" is our raison d'être. Since historians are so dependent upon library resources for their research and teaching, history librarians have a great deal of responsibility to educate this group in the best methods to find the materials that meet their information needs. As Booth also observed in the same article, "Teaching is hard." Teaching is hard and if it is to be done well, takes a great deal of knowledge and understanding of the subject, consultation with the course instructor, planning, and creativity. No one said library instruction for history classes was easy, particularly if the librarian has little experience either with history assignments or as an instructional librarian. Nevertheless, because historians and their students use the library as their laboratory, by teaching them the skills they need to negotiate your library, you are preparing them for a lifetime of research (even if it is not always on historical topics). Also, class size, learning objectives, and assignments change significantly from freshman level to senior. These changes become even more pronounced at the graduate level. New librarians need to develop an awareness to recognize when and where library instruction is appropriate and can be most effective, and when it may not be as important.

Many librarians devoutly believe every student should be given a thorough introduction to the library and its treasure troves of resources at every opportunity. This instruction could take the form of a fifty- or seventy-five-minute one-shot focusing on tips and skills needed to craft effective searches on a handful of specific databases, or it could take the guise of a required, credit-hour course designed to teach creative research and critical thinking skills students can take with them the rest of their lives. For better or worse, the one-shot seems to prevail. The idea of the librarian as tour guide leading a group of starry-eyed students to each of the main service points of the library building, as the students gaze in amazement at the wealth of resources now at their disposal, is still alive and well. We like to believe the polite fiction that these students will be hanging on our every word and their minds already dreaming up creative research projects based on this or that database or collection, which their omniscient librarian-guide is pointing out to them. Sometimes there is still a place for this kind of tour. However, we need to be aware that much of what we say will not be retained unless the students see an immediate assignment need, and the best that we can hope for is that they will at least remember where the library is on campus when they hit a wall in their first research assignment. For this reason, history librarians whose duties include instruction need to think about where and how one gets the most significant impact for time invested in the history curriculum. This chapter offers some ideas that will make this process easier for history librarians. For further discussion and some excellent ideas, see Jenny L. Presnell's *The Information-Literate Historian: A Guide to Research for History Students* (2007).

THE HISTORY CURRICULUM

As in other disciplines, history students begin with the very basic survey courses and slowly advance through progressively more specialized and narrowly focused courses. Although the introductory survey classes can be quite large in terms of enrollment numbers, advanced history students in upper-division courses are frequently limited to one or two dozen. Students who enter college with a high potential for scholastic aptitude may enroll in smaller honors courses (the exact designation will differ by school). Honors courses are much smaller than the introductory survey courses as a rule and often spend time examining topics to a much greater depth than is generally possible in other survey classes.

Survey Classes

It is an inconvenient truth that no one who cares about history likes to admit: many students' first, and frequently only, experience in a college-level history class is the introductory survey course. Often, these surveys are part of a general core curriculum that all students must take. At large universities, these can be huge classes, taught in immense auditorium lecture halls with one professor and half a dozen graduate assistants. At other institutions, these survey classes can be smaller and more intimate. In either case, however, the general learning objective is similar: introduce the students to the discipline by building a foundational knowledge of historical facts, dates, events, and people, all in their context and their importance to contemporary society. Depending on the institution, the main resources are a basic textbook and sometimes supplemental readings, usually snippets from important documents of the time. Similarly, these courses are often taught by non–tenure track faculty (lecturers, visiting or adjunct professors, and the like). In response to the sheer enrollment numbers and logistics, many of these classes use fact-based knowledge as the outcome and employ straightforward multiple choice/true-false exams that can be graded by a computer as their assessment measure. Even though historians claim that the teaching of critical thinking and effective writing skills have been their stock in trade for decades, and that higher education in general is making great strides in emphasizing critical thinking, writing, and communication skills as important parts of the curricula, the basic survey course has not effectively changed. Realistically, given a class of 200-plus students, and the need to cover anywhere from 150 to almost 5,000 years of historical material within the scope of a single, three-and-a-half month semester, the basic objective of acquainting these eighteen-year-old students with a timeline of important people and events from the time before they were born on a national or world stage takes precedence.

At smaller institutions or for special survey classes limited to intended history majors or other instances, one may be able to employ the "drive-by BI" technique mentioned by Arant-Kaspar and Benefiel, in which, with prior approval from the course instructor, one simply drops into a class in its regular meeting place and time, introduces oneself, passes out business cards, delivers a brief message of what the library has to offer, and then leaves (Arant-Kaspar and Benefiel 2008). This kind of session need not take up any more class time than five to ten minutes. Conversely, in the larger classes with students of all majors and classifications, where sheer numbers prevent any sort of inquiry-based assignments, the better library instruction method may be none at all with the resolution to focus on engaging the students later in their academic careers, when some of them will be in advanced history classes, with definite library resource needs.

Honors Designation

An exception to the large survey classes alluded to above is the honors course. The exact designation will vary by institution, but generally speaking these courses are limited both in size (often no more than two dozen) and/or enrollment profile (only the more academically accomplished students, or to intended majors only). These courses will often share the same course catalog number as the super-sized classes, but have a distinguishing section number or H descriptor (this will vary by institution). Because enrollment is capped at a much lower and more manageable number, the teaching methodology and assignments can be much more creative. Even at the freshman level, honors courses are often taught by senior faculty, often those recognized as the most inspiring teachers rather than lecturers or graduate assistants. The approach generally goes beyond basic names and dates to more creative, inquiry-based assignments. Particularly in history classes, this means introducing the students to primary source materials early and often. History librarians may be asked to conduct a library skills session to introduce the students to the library and the resources they need to find primary sources to complete their assignments. The assignments frequently begin small and get more complex as the semester advances.

An initial foray into primary source assignments for freshmen honors students often begins with having the students pick a topic based on the time period being covered, find a primary source from that time period, and write up a one- or two-page report describing that source and its historical context. By the end of the semester, these students may have advanced to longer (perhaps five-page) essays comparing and contrasting several primary sources on their chosen topics. History librarians should see this as an opportunity to engage with the instructors teaching these classes as to the potential contribution of a library instruction session. The instructor may have already handpicked the primary sources in order of consistency, relevancy, and importance, or to make sure the students have acceptable sources readily available. On the other hand, the instructor may welcome the opportunity to introduce the students to the wide range of resources available to them at the library.

Midlevel Coursework

History classes at the sophomore and junior level tend to be populated more with students who plan to major or minor in history (but there still may be some present just to meet a core curriculum requirement as well). They may not all go into history as a profession, but they are usually more interested in the field than a typical freshman who plans on being a physician or an engineer just like Mom or Dad. Other students in this level of classes may be those taking the courses as electives, but still, they typically have more than just a passing interest in the subject matter. During these courses, the pedagogy shifts from basic knowledge of facts and dates to more critical thinking about the causes and significance of events. The course materials become more complex as minority voices begin to come out of the wings and closer to center stage. As a rule, these classes are smaller than the typical U.S. History to 1877 survey course, thus allowing for more creative assignments. Examinations are less multiple-choice and more short-essay-type questions. The projects students will be working on will vary, but outside writing assignments generally include comparative analysis, reviews of particular books, a series of short (three pages) thought papers on a particular person, event, or issue, and/or a longer term paper of up to ten pages. Initially the instructors will focus more on secondary sources: books, book reviews, and scholarly journal articles. However, as the semester progresses some may begin requiring primary source materials. Since many institutions are beginning to require faculty to post syllabi online for student access, this makes it much easier to find and review them for opportunities to offer library instruction sessions. At large universities, these courses may still be too large to effectively include an independent research component, so librarians here may still not have much of an entrée into the classroom.

Senior-Level Coursework

Senior history majors at many institutions of higher education must write some form of capstone paper in order to complete their degree program requirements. Typically, these originate in senior-level seminar-style classes, which are often limited to no more than fifteen students and cover a very narrow topic in depth. Students generally have a much longer reading list from the available scholarly literature (mostly monographs) and their final research paper may exceed twenty pages. The use of primary source materials for these research papers is generally required. Because of the nature of these classes and the importance of a major research paper, history librarians should make it a point to contact the professors teaching these classes and offer library instruction sessions. There are exceptions such as professors taking a group of students out of the country for study-abroad experiences. In such cases, the research paper component may be very different than those who stayed home. A little detective work may be required to find out what faculty are teaching these capstone classes (you will probably be able to find out from departmental office staff or the undergraduate advisor as the new course schedule is being prepared). Contacting the professors teaching these senior seminars a few weeks prior to the posting of schedules and syllabi is often sufficient to secure a time and date when the class can be brought in for instruction (or if the library does not have sufficient classroom space, you the librarian may need to be prepared to meet the students in their classroom). If the library has recently acquired a new database that would be particularly useful for one of these classes, history librarians should be sure to mention it during their contact with the professors. For example, if a library has just acquired electronic access to ProQuest's *Acta Sanctorum* database, the history librarian should make sure the professor of medieval (or religious) studies is aware of this resource for her upcoming senior seminar class on Europe in the Early Middle Ages.

Graduate-Level Coursework

Even though graduate research seminars represent the preponderance of graduate coursework in history, there are a few special courses that do not follow this mold. One exception to the highly specialized graduate seminar classes is historiography. A course in historiography is generally required by most graduate programs. Historiography, as mentioned earlier, is the study of how history has been studied and written about from the distant past to the present. Students read examples of the earliest historical texts from Thucydides and Herodotus, to the most ground-breaking historical interpretations by present-day scholars. The course can also be an excellent place for history librarians to introduce themselves to a significant number of graduate students at once. While the professor may assume that the graduate students are already aware of and experienced with research using primary sources, you may need to remind the professor that a number of the students may have done undergraduate work at a different institution, and they may need an introduction to your library, its resources, and its services. If the professor seems hesitant to dedicate an entire class period to an introductory session, you could arrange for the "drive-by BI" mentioned above, which only takes a few minutes. You could make the offer to take appointments for individual orientations or research consultations, or if you plan on keeping an office hour, be sure to announce that fact.

Research Seminar–Style Courses

In many respects, graduate-level seminars resemble the senior seminar, except on a more professional scale. Graduate courses will generally have a required reading list of about a dozen scholarly monographs instead of a textbook or three. Rather than lectures on the topic by the professor, much of the class time is devoted to discussing the required readings, dissecting and debating how well the authors made their points, or critiquing how poorly they used the evidence. Graduate seminars typically have several in-depth reviews or critiques, either of required titles, or comparing other, similar works in the field. Additionally, there is generally a major research project in the form of a paper. This paper may eventually become a chapter in a student's thesis or dissertation, or it may serve as foundational material for the same. The student may also be looking to turn the finished research paper into a submission to a scholarly history journal. Whether destined to be a dissertation chapter or journal submission, the professor's expectations in terms of the quality and quantity of both the student's research and writing will be very, very high. Primary source materials form the core of the project, but the student must also demonstrate a significant familiarity with, and references to, the relevant scholarly literature on their chosen topic. At this level, successfully marketing library instruction sessions becomes somewhat challenging. While professors regularly recognize the need for students to learn about the library and available resources, there is also an expectation that most students will already have more than just a passing familiarity with the school's library. Even if the students did their undergraduate work at a different institution, professors may expect that the students will show the initiative to seek out this information on their own as part of their professional training. Students who recognize their need for help in the library are expected to seek out help on their own time. On the other hand, graduate students in history are often afforded a different level of treatment by professors. Frequently, there is the recognition that these students represent the next generation of professors. While this more collegial treatment very much depends on the individuals in question, professors generally assume more of a mentoring role. If a student needs help finding sources, the professor is sometimes more likely to try his own hand at working with the student, before turning a protégé over to librarians.

The topics covered by graduate seminars reflect the idea of preparing the next generation of scholars. The readings and resulting papers will very much resemble the topics mentioned in the first two chapters of this book. Today's graduate students are tomorrow's historians. They are expected to contribute new, original knowledge to the field: either by reexamining events covered by earlier historians with new understandings and theories of race and gender (for just two examples), or by truly breaking new ground and discovering heretofore undiscovered caches of sources, or untold stories of resistance to imperialist hegemony, and bringing these to the light of day. In order to better assist the next generation of scholars, history librarians need to be aware of the important issues and trends within the discipline of history, and thus be able to converse intelligently, and provide meaningful help to them.

Beyond the Basic Curriculum

Another method to increase awareness of library resources and yourself as a source of information and assistance in using library resources is to get involved with any new student orientations that might be held for incoming students (this is particularly effective at the graduate level). Similarly, there may be a student organization for history students (graduate, undergraduate, or both), and you could offer to attend one of the meetings or do a special program for a meeting. Phi Alpha Theta (http://phialphatheta.org) is the national honor society for history and there are chapters at colleges and universities across the country. Membership is generally limited to history majors because of the number of courses in history, as well as the high grades in those history classes, that are required for acceptance. In addition to Phi Alpha Theta, many departments sponsor history clubs for students of all majors who really like history, but may not plan to make a career of it. Meeting with these groups is a productive way to promote library resources and services, as well as yourself as being available to help.

HISTORY COMPONENTS IN OTHER DISCIPLINES

History librarians may be asked to contribute or assist with library instruction classes from other disciplines if the class has a historical focus. Generally, these will be upper-division courses for majors in that particular discipline, but not always. Sometimes these courses appear as "History of (discipline X)" in the course catalog, but because these are not history courses per se, the emphasis, assignments, and expectations will be different than what one normally finds in a history class. The topics can range widely, from an architecture course on Baroque style, to a political science course needing the historical background on the problems surrounding Arab-Israeli relations, to an interdisciplinary course examining the World Systems Theory of Immanuel Wallerstein and others. In such cases, primary sources may or may not be needed. Be sure to consult with the course instructors well in advance. They may simply want their students to know how to find scholarly material to set the context for their real discussion of the issues based on resources closer to their own fields. These classes are excellent opportunities to partner with another librarian to teach the session, but it helps things go much more smoothly if you and the other librarian work things out in advance regarding how much each person contributes and how to pass the focus back and forth during the session. It does happen that one librarian firmly believes that he must devote well over half of the time allotted to cover a single resource. This can create some difficulty in giving the students adequate instruction in the rest of the material, and can cause some frustration on the part of the course instructor. Clear communication between all parties regarding expectations, needs, resources, and teaching styles is absolutely essential for success. As long as everyone is on the same page, and as long as the librarians recognize that the course instructor, who is responsible for assessing the work the students turn in and assigning grades accordingly, is ultimately responsible for the conduct and content of the class and must have the final word on how sessions are run, the course should go smoothly.

Special Event Newspaper Assignment

A classic assignment that frequently appears at reference service desks over the years comes out of introductory journalism or communication classes (although history classes contributed their share as well): the students must find front-page headlines from their hometown newspaper on the day of their birth. Variations on this assignment included finding national or international stories in their hometown paper, or finding headlines from national and international newspaper titles from their birth date. Most librarians and library staff (especially those who used to work in the microfilm departments) have generally cringed thinking about the chaos created by this biannual ritual. While more on why this type of assignment is such a poor class activity will be discussed later in this chapter, suffice to say here that schools with limited holdings of microfilm newspapers, or large hordes of students (all about the same age) competing for the same few reels of microfilm in a narrow time window, or a school that attracts students from a wide geographical base but only holds a few selected microfilm newspapers, all of which may be national in scope, but nothing regional, will lose the goodwill of the students trying to complete the assignment.

There is some good news for libraries faced with this assignment: the full-text (and sometimes full-image) online sources for news from LexisNexis, Readex/NewsBank, and ProQuest help tremendously with this type of assignment. Having subscriptions to any of these online news sources can relieve much of the chaos of a mad rush for a single drawer in the microfilm cabinet, not to mention the wear and tear on the microfilm itself as well as the readers. Students can now search newspaper stories from their dorm rooms. These resources are not without some issues, however. Some students may not be able to find newspapers from their hometowns (especially those from small, rural communities). Finding a newspaper from the nearest metropolitan area that is both near the student's hometown and within the library's collection is usually an acceptable compromise. While electronic newspaper resources can show the students full-text articles from the newspapers on the date of their birth, particularly in the case of LexisNexis, that text is divorced from an image of the entire front page. While it may not seem important for some, there are professors (especially in journalism or similar fields) who consider where a story is placed on the page to be a statement of how important the newspaper editor thought that story to be. Articles appearing above the fold (where a newspaper is typically folded horizontally in half across the middle) are generally the leading stories of the day. Similarly, some databases provide text only and do not reproduce photographs, maps, charts, or other similar graphical material. Think of the impact of the headlines (often with a photograph) for the day the U.S. Space Shuttle *Challenger* exploded just moments after lift-off, or when Neil Armstrong stepped on the moon for the first time, or the now-famous picture of President Harry Truman holding up a newspaper that had printed its headline prematurely (and erroneously) declaring his defeat by his Republican rival. Providing only the intellectual content in the text of the articles themselves misses this important component and can undercut a critical part of the professor's educational objective.

BUILDING INSTRUCTIONAL PRESENTATIONS

One might assume from the previous discussion that there are so many variables going into each history class that there are no themes or resources in common. However, there are some components nearly all instruction sessions for a history class have that merit discussion here. So is there any such thing as a generic library instruction session for a history class and what goes into it? While the topics and specific assignments of the classes change, there are some common pieces of information that should be considered in most sessions. Although this list may seem excessive, you are teaching these students how to use what is essentially their laboratory. History is a library-intensive discipline and research in the field is heavily dependent on materials housed in libraries in many different formats, and with varied means of access and bibliographic control.

- **Contact information:** Your name, title, e-mail, and office phone number at minimum; if you use various social networking sites as part of your job, then mention those as well. This could be given as part of your introduction, but at the very least as part of your conclusion.

- **Primary sources defined:** A brief definition of primary sources with some examples from the library's collection. Historian Robin Winks has a particularly useful definition in the introduction to his book, *The Historian as Detective* (Winks 1969). The History Section of the ALA RUSA division also has an excellent discussion of primary sources on its website: http://www.ala.org/rusa/sections/history/resources/pubs/usingprimarysources. If the students will not have to use primary sources for any of their assignments in this class, this step can be omitted. You should work with the course instructor so your definition of primary sources will be compatible with the instructor's. Some professors may use a very narrow definition for the purposes of an individual assignment. If such is the case, remember the professors may have a pedagogical reason for what they do and it is not our job as librarians to undermine that strategy. If there is a more effective method, we can point that out with the recognition that it may or may not be accepted.

- **Local library's website:** Include a *brief* demonstration of how to navigate the library's website. Where is the link to the catalog? How does one find information about library hours? Where are the subject guides? Where is the link to interlibrary lending/borrowing services? Is there a link for basic FAQs (assuming this page has truly useful information from genuine frequently asked questions)?

- **Searching tips:** Truncation and Boolean operators make searching electronic resources more effective. You will need to emphasize to students looking for primary source materials that language changes over time and the search terms that quickly come to our modern minds may not be the terms used in full-text electronic resources such as *Early English Books Online*. A discussion of various euphemisms and alternate spellings may be required. The phrase "painted ladies" in an architectural history class would be interpreted as homes and buildings from the late nineteenth and early twentieth centuries that were brightly painted to accentuate highly embellished features (especially in San Francisco); in an entomology class, it is a butterfly. However, to social historians of the nineteenth century, "painted lady" was an often-used euphemism for prostitute (the phrase "unfortunate girl" carried similar moral indictment). Many students are also confused by the archaic print characters (such as the elongated "s" resembling an "f") that frequently appear in old printed works. While most companies producing databases where this and similar characters appear have tried to correct for it, optical character recognition (OCR) software does have its limitations and a word of caution is in order (better still if you can show them a graphic example in a document). You may also need to remind them that news traveled much more slowly in the past than it does in our hyper-wired society today. The date on which an event appeared in the *New York Times* from 1901 was dependent on many variables including how far and how fast the report traveled (could it have been telegraphed all of the way? or only part of the way?) and even when the paper went to press.

- **Catalog demonstration:** Depending on your local automated library system, show the students the basics of finding books by author, title, and keyword. Also mention using LCSH to narrow a search. Depending on the assignments given to the students and the size and available resources a library has, you may want to show the students how to find primary sources.

- **Important indexes to scholarly literature:** A brief demonstration on how to find the major bibliographic resources based on the nature of the course. Start with *America: History and Life* and/or *Historical Abstracts*, depending on the focus of the class. How can the students craft their topics for more efficient searching? How can they limit their results? How can they find the full text of an article (if it is not readily provided)? Other important resources (depending on your local holdings) include JSTOR, Project MUSE, the History Cooperative, IMB (*International Medieval Bibliography*), and so forth.

- **Finding and accessing primary sources:** This one is entirely dependent on the assignment given and your local resources; but when included, always emphasize quality. Keep in mind (and by all means remind the students!) that not all primary source materials in a library's collection are necessarily only available electronically. Some schools may be fortunate enough to have a subscription to one or more of ProQuest's historical newspapers online (including the *New York Times, Washington Post,* and *Christian Science Monitor*) or to Readex/Newsbank's *Early American Imprints* collection of books and pamphlets published in North America between 1639 and 1820. Librarians at schools with smaller budgets may have to be more creative. Keep in mind that there are many institutions such as the Library of Congress that make primary source material freely available on the Web. The American Memory project is an incredible digital museum of some real treasures from the collections of the Library of Congress (http://memory.loc.gov). Similarly, the Library of Congress is digitizing newspapers from more than twenty states between 1836 and 1922 http://chroniclingamerica.loc.gov). Once again, do not neglect your own print holdings. In most cases, a published diary such as *Mary Chesnut's Civil War* (edited by C. Vann Woodward), or a U.S. Department of Agriculture publication on preserving foods during wartime from the 1940s can be considered primary. Students in classes covering United States history in the nineteenth or twentieth centuries have two resources that grant them access to a wealth of popular periodical literature from those time periods (and thus, primary sources). *Poole's Index to Periodical Literature* by William Frederick Poole is an index to popular American magazines in the nineteenth century, while *The Reader's Guide to Periodical Literature* by H. W. Wilson (now available online via EBSCO) indexes popular and some scholarly magazines and journals for the twentieth century. Both of these resources are now available online and librarians instructing students who need primary materials for these time periods should not overlook these important gateways into the literature of the times. Librarians whose institutions do not have electronic access may still have print copies in the stacks, and could supplement them with free electronic access to the joint *Making of America* project of nineteenth-century periodicals and books by the University of Michigan and Cornell University (http://moa.umdl.umich.edu).

- **Conclusion:** Wrap up, remind the students of your contact information, and invite questions.

This outline can be altered depending on the nature of the assignments, level of the class, class size, and instructor goals. Likewise, there is nothing that says the order cannot be changed to fit local needs or circumstances. For example, if the class is a small group of honors freshmen who have never yet set foot in the campus library, a walking tour pointing out some of the various service points might be in order. Walking tours could also be effective for a group of new graduate students, especially if few of them did their undergraduate work at your institution. Other variations on these steps might include having the students participate in searches either on their own laptop computers, or in a computer lab. You may design your presentation in such a way as to include questions to the students, who then respond via clickers and an interactive scoreboard projected in the room. One thing for certain, the future will bring additional resources, some of which will truly assist librarians in their responsibilities as educators; others will soon be forgotten as mere gadgets, toys, and fads. Helping the students become more proficient researchers in the library across various formats will always remain a priority. Although it is not within the scope of this book to cure you of stage fright, successful instructional sessions are dependent on being aware of how you behave when speaking before a group. Unless you can rely on colleagues for feedback, you may want to spend time practicing (perhaps even with a video camera) to make sure your articulation is understandable and you can limit any distracting habits (such as dropping your voice near the end of a sentence or fidgeting with your wristwatch).

Fifty minutes goes by a lot faster than you might expect, so you will want to practice your delivery to make sure you can touch on the important points. Always keep in mind what resources the course instructor wanted to emphasize and organize your presentation around those (especially if they have recently been converted to electronic format). Do not get bogged down on the nuances of your favorite database, or pontificating on the intricacies of esoteric metadata. A fifty-minute session, or even a seventy-five-minute session for classes meeting twice per week, is only enough time to cover the basics and hopefully whet the appetites of students who might want to dig deeper. You will certainly want to take questions during and shortly after the class period, but it is also quite sensible to invite interested students to meet with you via appointment at a later time.

COLLABORATIVE PARTNERING ON ASSIGNMENTS

You may have the opportunity to work with a history faculty member to design better library assignments. Elements of good library assignments will be different depending on the class, size, level of difficulty of the associated course assignment, and educational objectives of the course instructor. The recommendations here are intentionally vague so you can pick and choose which elements work best for you. Keep in mind that not all elements must be used in every session, and you may want to make some features available via social networking for later (depending on your technological abilities and organizational computing infrastructure). A good library assignment

- has clearly stated goals and objectives;
- has goals and objectives that can be met within the specified time frame and with the available library resources (this one will look very different depending on class level and size);
- is based on sound pedagogical methods;
- is logically and specifically relevant to the course;
- relates to other course-specific tasks;
- is preceded by adequate instruction in library skills (especially targeting the specific resources needed to complete the assignment);
- allows the students a reasonable amount of choice in selecting topics or sources given the course parameters; and
- bonus: teaches research, evaluation, and critical thinking skills the students can use in other courses and for the rest of their lives. (Grassian and Kaplowitz 2009; Mosley 1998)

Remember that the course instructor is ultimately responsible for giving the students the assignments and assessing their performance, not you (unless, of course, you are specifically asked to do so). Our role as librarians is to facilitate teaching and research, not act as the pedagogical police. Working with faculty can be (and often is) a rewarding and positive experience for everyone involved, but it does take some degree of diplomacy and tact as you work out the educational goals and objectives. Sometimes you may just have to do the best you can, show the students the printed indexes, and work with Dr. Smith on the library's electronic version of his favorite database for next semester.

INTERVENTION WITH THE INSTRUCTOR

There are times when faculty give poorly conceived assignments to students. Sadly this lapse in pedagogy is not limited to history faculty, nor is it limited only to inexperienced faculty members. Poor assignments can be given to any class, regardless of class level or size. When this happens in a history class or a class with significant historical content, and the students show up at the library for assistance, you (as history librarian) may have to get involved. Depending on the issues at hand, you may need to contact the instructor responsible for giving the assignment.

Poor assignments come in many guises. Often, the course instructor sends the students to use a resource that the library does not have. Perhaps the instructor used a specific resource at the institution where she earned her doctorate, or perhaps she has misremembered a given source's content and believes it has useful information when it actually does not. Perhaps the instructor is not aware that the required resource at your library has been converted to electronic format (the reverse may also be true: the instructor is familiar with the electronic, but your library only has the print). Whatever the specifics of the situation, the end result is that the assignment requires the students to use a source that your library does not have. What was true in the previous section on collaborating with faculty regarding diplomacy and tact is just as applicable here. When students begin overrunning the reference desk (or the queues in virtual reference chat sessions have become unmanageable), you may need to contact the instructor who issued the assignment and apprise him of the situation. If it is only an issue of print versus electronic format of a specific resource, explaining to the instructor that his preferred means of access does not exist, and offering to teach the class how to use the format the library owns, may be all that is required. If the instructor has required the students to use a resource not owned in any format, you will need to be familiar enough with multiple resources to offer a resource within your library that gives similar information (this is where being knowledgeable about your library's history collection pays off). Dealing with faculty on this type of issue is not always easy or pleasant. Sometimes you may have to bite your tongue as you endure some pithy comments about how much better the collections were at their previous institution's library. Such comments, though painful at the time, could provide the impetus for discussions on improving your library's interlibrary lending services, or looking at joining consortia such as the Center for Research Libraries. However, those enhancements are not cheap or easily made, and will do little to help the floundering students in this semester's class. Sometimes database providers will give a library temporary, trial access to a database for a limited time. Generally, the understanding is that the library is seriously considering the resource for purchase or subscription. However, sometimes these database trials can be set up so that the students can access the necessary material for the given assignment. Nevertheless, this practice should be the exception and not the rule as it sometimes creates an unreasonable expectation of purchase of the resource by the library. Keep in mind that this is the instructor's class, not ours. The instructor may decide to write off the assignment and take it off the syllabus, or ask if you can present an alternative source to change the requirement regarding using a specific database, or otherwise alter the assignment. There are times when a large class is required to use a given resource that overwhelms the limited number of simultaneous users for that resource. Oftentimes your database provider can temporarily increase the number of simultaneous users with little or no charge, but perhaps a reassessment regarding the number of users you are paying for will be in order.

Because the large survey classes can be taught by instructors with limited teaching experience, there are occasions when a poorly conceived library assignment turns into an opportunity for liaison librarians to get involved, promote library services, or even schedule a visit with the class. One example of such a situation may be that an instructor asks the students to write a review of a particular book title. Rather than give the students (mostly freshmen, for this example) detailed directions and descriptions of their expectations, the instructor simply says, "go to the library and find a book review and use that as a template." A couple of days before the assignment is due, 150 students begin to descend on the reference desk demanding book reviews of history books, completely overwhelming the unprepared staff. This is frequently when the history librarian will first hear of such an assignment. It will take some cooperation between the desk staff and the librarian to track down which instructor gave the assignment (don't be surprised if many students' response is "I'm in History 151; no, I don't know which section"). In addition to perseverance, this situation also calls for a considerable amount of tact and diplomatic skill on the librarian's part. It is highly unprofessional to discuss how bad an assignment is with the student to whom it has been given. Such talk foments a lack of respect and turns the student against the instructor. Also, many inexperienced instructors may be a bit insecure in their role and may be more than a little defensive if their pedagogy is questioned. Conversely, experienced instructors are not immune to this either, and it may well be that the person who gave the poor assignment is a respected senior faculty member. Remember what I just mentioned about tact and diplomatic skills? You may need to carefully consider what you say and how you say it (and frequently use the "delete" key before sending that inflammatory e-mail). Many professors see pedagogy as an integral part of their academic freedom and no one is going to tell them why they cannot give the same assignment they have given for decades. If you are lucky, it may only be a case of suggesting that the old printed resource to which the students were sent has been superseded by an electronic version. In our example above of finding book reviews, perhaps the instructor could delay the due date a week and let you come into the class and give a brief demo of JSTOR, Project MUSE, and *America: History and Life*. Most people do not intentionally make trouble for the library and are willing to accept some gentle coaching and compromise.

TOO MUCH OF A GOOD THING?

Is it possible to have too much of a good thing? Like so many things in life, there is a point where "more" is no longer better, it is just "too much." This truism applies to library instruction as well. There will come a point where you reach population saturation; you walk into a classroom, you have a scintillating presentation with all the bells, whistles, and animated graphics, and you are ready to give the students the lessons they need to become information-savvy and efficient library researchers; but then you realize you recognize most of the students in the room. Some of them were in an instruction session you did for a different history professor last week. Other students were in a class yet another professor brought into the library the previous semester. Uh-oh, these students have seen your presentations, they have heard your jokes (some even laughed), some of them worked with you face-to-face to find sources for their papers. What now? At this point, flexibility is your greatest asset. You may want to ask by show of hands how many students have already been through one of your sessions. If all but a handful raise their hands, you need to be willing to pitch your script. Some parts you keep, namely those relating to databases unique to this particular course subject (especially if the interface of an important database has recently changed). However, if the students can answer some questions regarding what primary sources are and give some good examples, that part of your presentation may be dropped (unless the instructor steps in to request a refresher). You might consider offering the students who have not seen your presentation the chance to meet with you at another time to go over that material in more detail and spend the scheduled class period working with new resources, letting the students work on their own (whether on library laptop computers, their own laptops, or by moving into a computer lab or hands-on instruction room).

Collaboration with the course instructor ahead of time can reduce the surprise effect of entering the classroom prepared for one type of audience and finding another. Enlist the instructor's assistance in determining how much instruction may be needed and on which topics. Perhaps the course instructor could help by going over some basic material before bringing the class into the library; the two of you could work on definitions and examples of primary sources that would be especially relevant to this class. This way you can concentrate your efforts on helping the students with developing the skills needed to effectively use the sources on their topics. It can be more useful to devote much of the scheduled class time to allowing the students to search the libraries' resources (print and electronic) while you and the professor stand available for questions and assistance. Conversely, sometimes the professor has particular databases in mind that you should include in your presentation. A professor may similarly believe that even if many of the students have heard the material before, there are enough that have not (or who have not convinced the instructor that they understand it) to warrant a reinforcing session. Flexibility and being willing to work with the course instructor toward her pedagogical goals will ultimately help the most.

Scheduling Issues

When is the best time to schedule a library instruction session? Conventional wisdom would suggest bringing the students into the library at every opportunity and constantly barraging them with information on library resources at every turn. However, there is also a case to be made for just-in-time instruction, which leaves the students a much shorter window between the instructional session and when the related assignment is due. As much as we might like to believe ourselves to be scintillating lecturers who hold the students in rapt attention, or we are so suave and hip that we had the students dancing to our beat, it may be humbling to realize that many students will not remember much about what sources we used or what tips and shortcuts we demonstrated. These students will be contacting us shortly before the assignment is due (and "shortly" is a relative term, ranging from two weeks to just a few hours prior) and asking for refreshers on which database(s) to use, and how to craft the best search for relevant materials. *C'est la vie!* On the other hand, if you bring the students into the library with a shorter window, they can see a more immediate need for what we are trying to teach them, and thus retain more of what we say and do regarding resources and effective search strategies. Which method is better? There may not be one best way that works for every class. You are recommended to try both.

CONCLUSION

Whether it goes by the term *library instruction,* or *information literacy,* teaching library research skills to history students is a very challenging, yet quite rewarding, part of being a history librarian. Because the students are so dependent upon library resources for their research, assistance in navigating the system and crafting better searches is almost always greatly appreciated. For librarians, having greater knowledge and understanding of what is expected of the students will bear many benefits in terms of more relevant examples and meaningful materials. Working in close conjunction with the teaching faculty member, librarians can put together sessions as sophisticated and interactive or as simple and direct as fits the need. Librarians should remember that the instructor is ultimately responsible for assessing student performance and should not undercut the instructor's learning objectives. On the other hand, librarians can use these sessions to open up new worlds and new resources to the students that might inspire some to great feats of inquiry (it could happen). In designing a library instruction session, keep in mind the assignment the students are working on and do not forget that many intriguing and useful sources may not be electronic, but are found in the library's print collection. At the same time, electronic resources such as *American Periodicals Series Online* or *Making of the Modern World* or *Early American Imprints* can inspire students to immerse themselves in primary research. Each type of resource has its role to play, and depending on your library's holdings, each may serve as the spark to which a student responds. Some students may be completely taken with the ability to read online materials created decades (if not centuries) prior, while others may connect with a book that has survived many generations and has the worn feel and leathery smell from another time. These students are waiting for you as history librarian to open the doors for them.

6

DEFINING THE
HISTORY COLLECTION

History materials come in a wide variety of types and formats and there are issues associated with each, of which librarians for history must be acutely aware. Whether your title includes "selector," or "bibliographer," or something else, if part of your job responsibilities include managing the history collections within your organization, this chapter will hopefully be useful to you. Keep in mind that there are occasions when librarians who have "history" in their title are assumed to be archivists, curators, or similar specialists, which can cause some confusion and consternation for patrons. A patient explanation and referral to the correct person generally solves the issue. In trying economic times, librarians frequently find themselves wearing many hats, and instruction, reference, liaison, collection management, and perhaps even cataloging could ostensibly be placed on one person's head. Though it can frequently lead to confusion, responsibilities in some combination of these main fields is more likely the norm.

CHALLENGES OF HISTORY TO COLLECTION DEVELOPMENT POLICIES

A collection development policy is simply a written document that describes a particular portion of a library's collection and acts as something of a road map to guide current and future selection decisions. Collection development policies and procedures are must-haves in terms of operational and procedural guidelines. However, these guidelines must be flexible and not treated as carved-in-stone commandments that allow no provision for exceptions or the ability for occasional opportunistic acquisitions. History, because of its very nature, presents some unique challenges to rigid interpretation of collection policies, which will be discussed in more detail in the next chapter. Suffice here to say that narrowly defining history materials by a narrow range of call numbers or formats will adversely affect the collection because many important materials may be passed over. Materials useful to historians will be found throughout call number ranges. While you will want to take a broad and open-minded approach when drafting the collection policy, do remember that it should reflect the educational goals of your institution. How many books on European colonialism in Polynesia do you *really* need, if your institution has nothing in the curricula about it?

An earlier chapter covered reference materials and finding resources. The types that will generally constitute a main history collection in libraries include: monographs, serials, media, websites, and other specialty formats such as microforms. While historians also make extensive use of rare book, manuscript, and other types of archival materials, those require special care and considerations beyond the scope of this book. Each type of material has its own set of considerations for use by historians. Many of these sources can be purchased as either print or electronic, each with their own set of inherent advantages and disadvantages.

Monographs and the "Print v. e-Book" Issue

As mentioned in earlier chapters, the monograph is the primary form of scholarly communication for historians. This was documented by Margaret F. Stieg during the course of her study of scholarly historical periodicals when she was informed that "[historians] write books . . . not articles" (Stieg 1986). In order for informed discourse to occur, the historian must be aware of the often intricate subtleties that make up a colleague's argument, which requires a very close reading of the text. Therefore, history librarians with selector responsibilities are encouraged to favor print titles over electronic books in collection development policies. On a related note, you should be very cautious about discarding print copies of books in favor of electronic copies for just this reason. One practice that must be taken into consideration by the history librarian is that historians tend to read monographs cover-to-cover at a much deeper and more critical level than your average undergraduate student. Many e-book publishers or distributors severely limit the number of pages that can be viewed sequentially or printed in a single access session for copyright reasons. While an undergraduate needing only a choice quote or two while finishing a paper at 3:00 A.M. may be quite satisfied with the electronic version of a title, the historian wishing to read the book for more of its content, the author's thesis and use of evidence, and endnote referrals, will need a physical copy. To meet the historians' needs, librarians should consider simply purchasing a second, print copy to be less burdensome than dealing with the morass of modern copyright issues and imposed copyright limitations. Similarly, interlibrary lending (ILL) requests will often need the entire book rather than one or two chapters. For other materials, such as serials or scanned images, electronic delivery to the desktop can be a highly preferred format, as long as the scanning is of sufficient quality, contrast, and resolution. Charts, tables, graphs, maps, and photographs within those articles must be scanned with sufficient contrast and resolution for ease of use, rather than assumed to be used as text-only.

Even though they may not be the most desired format for cover-to-cover readability, scholarly monographs in history have been published electronically and librarians should be aware of this developing trend. NetLibrary (now part of EBSCO) books are well known and offer a wide selection of e-books by top-quality publishers (including university presses) on a variety of topics to libraries, even as the reader interface can be a barrier to effective use. However, in 1999, a joint venture between the AHA and Columbia University Press with backing from the Andrew Mellon Foundation resulted in Gutenberg-e (http://www.gutenberg-e.org). Gutenberg-e is an innovative project that takes some of the best dissertations and publishes them as electronic books. Authors are encouraged to take advantage of computers' capabilities, including the use of multimedia and hypertext links. The books are chosen based on broad subject categories for a given year. In that inaugural year, the topics were: Africa, colonial Latin America, and South Asia. Each year the topics change; and since its inception, books on Europe prior to 1800, military history and foreign relations, North America prior to 1900, and history of gender have been published. On one hand, these books are quite reasonable in price; on the other, there are issues still needing resolution including copyright, interlibrary loan, and printing. Also in 1999, the American Council of Learned Societies (ACLS), assisted by a Mellon Foundation grant, began a project to electronically publish important books in history. What began as the ACLS History E-Book project has expanded to include other humanities topics. As of mid-2011, the ACLS Humanities E-Book (HEB) (http://www.humanitiesebook.org) contained some three thousand titles. Some of these titles were in the public domain after the original copyright expired, but many are current titles recently published by contemporary scholars. Pricing is by subscription and ACLS bases its rates on number of full-time enrolled students and Carnegie classification (i.e., research institutions will be charged higher rates than nonresearch institutions). How well these electronic book projects are accepted by the historical community for research and teaching as well as for credit toward promotion and tenure remains to be seen, but history librarians will want to be aware that these options exist. On the other hand, unlike printed copies, which can be checked out and read at home by noninstitutionally affiliated community users, e-books would have to be used within the confines of the library's computer network.

DEFINING *SCHOLARLY* AND *HISTORICAL*

University Presses and Commercial Publishers

As explained elsewhere in this book, academic historians, like other scholars, desire monographs from scholarly publishers. Generally, this means university presses, although there are a number of commercial publishing companies that publish books often classified as history. It would be impractical (if not impossible given that some scholarly presses have banded together in consortia agreements) to list every university press here. Both R. R. Bowker and Gale-Cengage publish directories for the book trade. However, it does bear mentioning that there is a definite perceived pecking order or hierarchy in terms of quality. The university presses of Oxford, Cambridge, Harvard, and Yale are typically the gold standard, which most scholars in history (and many other disciplines) aspire to have publish their research. While it is generally safe to assume that the more prestige attached to a university, the more prestigious its press, there are exceptions. Librarians must keep in mind that many university presses concentrate on publishing books on local and regional topics (which can win coveted national-level awards) in addition to specializing in a few specific topics covering a wider geographical area. While Louisiana State University may have a reputation as a school focused more on its championship football team, the press is quite prestigious in the fields of Southern history and literature. Does a given university have an established program in a particular field (such as Islamic history)? If so, the press may tap into that local expertise to edit or assist with finding manuscripts of high quality. If the press is publishing a monographic series around a common theme, who is the series editor? If that person is a renowned author, the quality of the books in that series will probably be quite high. Looking to see who sits on the press's editorial board is another factor to consider in judging quality. High-quality books about the American West based on meticulous scholarly research are frequently published by such geographically diverse universities as Yale, Texas, and Stanford. Similarly, Kansas University Press will publish quality books on such diverse topics as local and Midwestern history, military history, and American studies. Fortunately, most university presses now have their catalogs available online, which (along with more general Internet search engines) can make tracking down the latest book on 1970s labor history in Detroit that Dr. Jones wants to use for her class next semester much easier.

Many approval plan vendors allow a university press delineation. However, there is a caveat regarding university presses that needs to be made. Not all books from university presses are scholarly. As university presses have fallen victim to budget crises, and experienced the need to appeal to a broader audience, many have taken to publishing books that may have much more appeal to an audience outside of academia's cloistered halls. These may be good books on flora and fauna of the state for hikers, or about regional popular culture, but more likely these titles will not have the scholarship and documentation behind them that most history faculty want to see their students use. Similarly, there have been instances where otherwise respectable university presses have republished works in the public domain with slightly altered author and/or title attributions. While perhaps not intentionally done to deceive, unsuspecting libraries relying strictly on approval plans for collection building may essentially find themselves with multiple copies of the same collection of pioneer women's diaries from the nineteenth century. On the other hand, if your library's original copy has gone missing or worn out, or your library never had a copy of this material, buying these reprints is a good way to pick up appropriate books for the history collection.

Although university press-published titles are generally thought to be of higher quality by many, some trade publishers such as Hill and Wang (a division within Farrar, Straus, and Giroux, an imprint of Macmillan) publish history books of very high quality, written by respected historians. Nevertheless, librarians need to be aware there are some concerns that must be mentioned regarding commercial publishing houses. Because commercial companies publish a wide variety of books that appeal to a large audience with varying levels of education and sophistication, there are numerous books that may appear to be of historical interest, but are not scholarly and should be treated with caution.

History Pretenders

Many popular authors will write nonfiction accounts of historical topics. While these books are entertaining, and may even be supported by documentary evidence, they are not considered scholarly and are of very limited value to professional historians. These often best-selling titles range from the tragic 1900 Galveston, Texas, hurricane to gritty and graphic true crime stories. These books may make for pleasurable reading by an armchair historian, but they rarely engage deeper or larger issues that academic historians, as well as their students, must address. Also to be treated with caution are titles dealing with current events, politics, or current military situations, such as in the Middle East. While many of these are well written and may be based on some degree of research, others are little more than partisan polemics. The reason this warning is included here is because many of these books are being assigned call numbers that traditionally classify these titles as history in approval plans (i.e., LCCN C-F or Dewey 900s). It can be argued that at some point in the future, some historian examining the heated, partisan rhetoric that was consumed by and captivating to people living in the late twentieth and early twenty-first centuries may have an interest in reading these books, but this argument is speculative. Librarians must have a rational and defensible reason (preferably linked to an obvious teaching or research need) for either including or excluding these titles from a collection.

In addition to books on current events masquerading as history, there are other categories of history-like topics that must be treated with caution. There is a genre within the Holocaust denial literature that attempts to cloak itself with respectability and marks of legitimate scholarship. Generally, close inspection will reveal its true nature, but this does require a degree of vigilance that many find difficult to maintain consistently. This genre and other variations of conspiracy theories abound and take on historical topics such as the Kennedy assassinations, UFOs at Roswell, New Mexico, hidden treasures or secret plans aboard the *Titanic* or other sunken ships, Masonic rituals throughout history, and hidden messages within Da Vinci's written notes. Librarians must be aware that while much of it might be popular (even to the point of being made into major motion pictures), much of this literature is of little use to academic historians. In addition to these examples of popular history, pseudo-history, or quasi-history, forgeries and faked documents exist as well as other documents certain people may wish were faked (Gracy 2001; Groneman and Crisp 1995; Sowards 1988). Unfortunately, refusing to purchase these materials on ideological grounds alone opens one to the charge of censorship and violations of freedom of speech. Careful wording in the collection policy statements and setting of approval profiles to align with departmental research and teaching support can prevent wasting precious resources on this material. On the other hand, if there is an institutional need, such as a faculty member's research or courses being taught on these kinds of subjects, then selecting carefully chosen titles with cautious cataloging and classification may be in order. History librarians must also be aware that language and sensibilities change over time and older material may contain language that our modern and enlightened society considers offensive for a variety of reasons (ethnic, gender, sexual orientation, etc.). For historians examining issues of discrimination, these can be excellent and legitimate sources. Librarians must be just as careful about what they choose to exclude from their collection as what they choose to include in their collection.

Disgraceful Withdrawal?

Another cautionary statement must be made regarding books written by professional historians and scholars that are later shown to be false or otherwise deeply flawed. A case in point is Michael A. Bellesiles's book, *Arming America: The Origins of a National Gun Culture*, published in 2000 by the otherwise respectable trade publisher, Alfred A. Knopf. As if the book's thesis were not controversial enough (that most Americans in the eighteenth and nineteenth centuries were not nearly as familiar and adept with firearms as our foundational myths claim), an even greater firestorm erupted when scrutiny of Bellesiles's sources failed to validate his claims. Bellesiles resigned from a tenured position at a respected university in disgrace (Robin 2004). The issue for librarians now becomes: what to do with this book? Should it be withdrawn from the shelves and de-accessioned? Or should it be retained, to be used as an example of how professional history should *not* be researched and written? Of course, it was only after the book's publication that the controversy broke out. Given the reliance on approval plans by so many libraries, quite a number of copies are currently sitting on shelves. According to a WorldCat search performed in July 2011, more than two thousand libraries worldwide held a copy. The question of what to do when a student or faculty member brings the library's copy to your attention, wanting it to be withdrawn or recataloged as fiction, may be worth having a discussion. Altering your collection development policies is probably unnecessary as such cases are assumed to be the exceptions and not the rule. Pulling books from shelves is a slippery slope that can quickly move into issues of censorship, partisanship, and professional ethics.

TEXTBOOK CONSIDERATIONS

Textbooks, especially within the discipline of history, can be problematic. Many libraries are struggling with issues of whether to purchase copies of course textbooks for the collection or not. While these materials would undoubtedly be used, how much space in the stacks a given library can devote to a collection of this nature merits serious consideration. New librarians for history may be asked to contribute to these discussions, although sometimes the policy on whether to have a textbook collection is decided at a higher level. One important issue of which history librarians should be aware is that in junior-, senior-, and graduate-level history classes, the assigned readings more often than not include scholarly monographs that may or may not be classified as a textbook (or even a history book!) by the publisher or approval plan vendor. The 1991 book *When Jesus Came the Corn Mothers Went Away: Marriage, Sexuality, and Power in New Mexico, 1500–1846* by Ramón A. Gutiérrez and published by Stanford University Press provides an excellent case in point. This prestigious award-winning book is often assigned as a textbook in classes ranging from Borderlands, Native American Studies, Mexican Studies, Religious Studies, Women's Studies, and History of the American Southwest, despite having an LCCN of HQ 835 (Divorce). It also finds its way into the bibliographies of many scholarly works as an important book in the field that scholars must consult in order to address the complex issues Gutiérrez brought forth. A librarian's thorough knowledge of the courses being taught and assigned readings on the syllabi is a real asset in choosing materials in these situations. Conversely, should a library decide against building a textbook collection, new librarians for history must be equally aware that some monograph titles may be blocked in approval plans just because they happened to be listed as textbooks or appear on a course reading list, and prevent this exclusion if possible.

Generally speaking, a textbook will usually have multiple authors or an editor, whereas, just as the name implies, a historical monograph will only have one author. Unfortunately, *Festschriften* (a book published in honor of a major scholar with essays contributed by that person's former students) are sometimes incorrectly classified as textbooks, as are scholarly collected works. Often, these collections of essays are more useful to students because an essay tends to be shorter and easier to read, and hits the most important points in a form that is easier to follow than an entire monograph by the same author. Occasionally these books are useful to teaching faculty from which to draw supplemental reading assignments as well. You should not have any qualms about adding books of this type from reputable publishers to their collection.

SERIALS

Scholarly journals in history, like scholarly journals in other disciplines will often require attention. While the monograph is the primary method of scholarly communication among historians, journals still play an important role. Although many libraries are cutting journal subscriptions, there may be some libraries with the resources to add new titles after canceling others or even establish new subscriptions outright. A small consolation is that most journals in history, like many other humanities titles, are much less expensive than titles in physics, chemistry, or the medical sciences. Many history journals are still published by the professional organization that sponsors the journal. However, the American Historical Association (AHA) recently announced it was turning over publication of its journal, the *American Historical Review*, to the University of Chicago Press. The AHA is not alone and there are a number of scholarly journals in history published by major university presses such as Duke University and Johns Hopkins University. Although not as common, there are a few historical journals that are published by commercial publishers such as Blackwell. Libraries that maintain institutional memberships in various professional organizations often get the organization's journal and even a newsletter as a part of that membership. Since these institutional memberships are generally much more expensive than individual memberships (although history journals remain quite a bargain compared to other disciplines), the costs and benefits must be seriously considered when evaluating serials either for purchase or cancellation. Even without membership status, journal subscriptions for institutions are much more expensive than subscriptions for individuals.

Journals in Electronic Format

New librarians for history need also to be aware of the availability of scholarly serials through electronic means. Part of this discussion harkens back to the blurring of the line between reference sources that previously provided only bibliographic control to periodical literature with those resources that now provide full text. Companies such as EBSCO and H. W. Wilson (which at the time of this writing just announced a merger under the EBSCO banner) are providing an increasing amount of full-text serials in the field of history. There are also the JSTOR, http://www.jstor.org, and Project MUSE, http://muse.jhu.edu, journals offering full text and full image so almost no information from the original journal is lost. JSTOR is a nonprofit organization providing an electronic archive of more than 250 of the most important journals in the field of history as well as numerous other journals in a myriad of disciplines. Until 2011, JSTOR did not offer access to the most recent five years of a journal's title and only contained retrospective collections. However, with the Current Scholarship Program, JSTOR is providing access to current material for a much more limited selection of its total number of titles. There are also additional initiatives with JSTOR, including full-text books and even some primary source collections. Project MUSE, on the other hand, has fewer history and more literary titles, but readers will find the most recent articles from the journal, though it only has holdings for the past fifteen years or so. The History Cooperative, http://www.historycooperative.org, a joint venture between the AHA, OAH, the University of Illinois Press, and the National Academies Press, gives members of the participating professional organizations, as well as libraries with print subscriptions, access to the full text of the most recent issues of almost two dozen major journals in history.

Many journals, especially those from large, national organizations, as well as university or commercial publishers, are now available electronically. However, these resources offer only a small percentage of the total number of journals in history; generally speaking, they are limited only to major journals of broad national interest. Also, librarians should be cognizant of the unique features, benefits, and liabilities associated with each service. Many smaller state historical journals or niche journals do not have the resources to publish in this format. It may be that these smaller, niche titles are not considered to have a broad enough market to be economically attractive for converting to digital publishing. Regional research institutions should make every effort to collect serial publications from historical associations and societies in the surrounding area if space and money permit. National research institutions have the similar duty to collect local and regional resources from within their immediate geographic locale as the largest repository in the area (the presence of active, well-funded regional historical societies, public archives, or smaller research universities can reduce the burden of responsibility, though it may require more communication and collaboration among the different entities).

Defining Top-Tier Journals in History

New history librarians should familiarize themselves with the top journals for the discipline at the national, international, as well as state and local levels. The ISI database "Web of Knowledge," by Thomson Reuters (http://thomsonreuters.com) has the "Journal Citation Reports" feature, which not only lists the top journals in a particular broad field (history is included as a social science), but also offers quantitative rankings based on several criteria. Keep in mind that this looks at the field very broadly, and at an international level. Highly influential and respected state historical journals, or journals with a much narrower focus (time period, geographical region, or topic) rarely appear. Within scholarly journals for history, much of every issue is taken up with book reviews written by specialists in the field. Stieg points out that historians value the extensive lists of critical book reviews so much that practically every journal issue contains more pages for reviews than articles. Through these reviews, historians comment on the quality of work being done in their field and some historians use positive reviews of their books to strengthen their case for tenure and/or promotion. Many historians depend on these reviews to keep abreast with new works within their area of specialization (Stieg 1986).

Another consideration regarding history journals is the audience for each journal. Despite the title *American Historical Review*, articles within this premier journal are not limited just to topics relating to North America. Articles from the 2011 issues exemplify this trend and run the gamut from popular music's influence on the formation of Argentinean identity between 1895 and 1915, to narcotics trafficking in the Middle East between 1919 and 1939, to early Cold War efforts by the Soviet Union to bring former colonized regions into its sphere of influence. Conversely, the *Journal of American History*, published by the Organization of American Historians (OAH), is limited to articles relating to U.S. history. But even this reflects the changes in the discipline, as articles appearing in sample 2010 issues include a discussion on the meaning of terrorism in American history and an article on breast-feeding and maternal ideals between 1750 and 1860. Additional titles you may wish to consult are the following:

- *Agricultural History*
- *American Historical Review*
- *Annales*
- *British Journal for the History of Science*
- *Business History*
- *Environmental History*
- *Ethnohistory*
- *History Workshop Journal*
- *Isis*

- *Journal of African History*
- *Journal of African American History*
- *Journal of American History*
- *Journal of Economic History*
- *Journal of Historical Geography*
- *Journal of Interdisciplinary History*
- *Journal of Modern History*
- *Journal of Social History*
- *Journal of Southern History*
- *Labour History*
- *Past and Present*
- *Technology and Culture*
- *Western Historical Quarterly*
- *William and Mary Quarterly*
- *Zeitgeschichte*

Subscription-Based, Full-Text Primary Source Electronic Resources

In this digital age more and more primary source materials are made available in full text electronically with varying degrees of effectiveness in search and retrieval. Though not journals per se, the recurring maintenance cost model bears a similarity from the budgetary perspective. Because of this, the differentiation of the word *databases* as reference materials vis-à-vis *electronic resources* has become quite fuzzy. Even as major indexes were discussed earlier in chapter 4, there are many digitized collections that are useful to historians but may or may not be classified by the vendor or library administration as an index/database. As more and more resources that were originally published in print migrate to electronic format through retrospective conversion, and provide much more information than a simple bibliographic citation, separation by format and level of access almost seem moot. Having access to major electronic collections of primary documents holds many benefits for historical scholars, especially the ability to examine these materials without extensive travel. Examining a rare book or manuscript collection once meant the scholar had to go to the repository, whether that entailed a trip across town or across an ocean. Electronic resources such as *Early English Books Online (EEBO)* from ProQuest/Chadwyck-Healey can allow historians and their students to look at books printed between the fifteenth and eighteenth centuries in their entirety, with all the illustrations and eccentric print characters from their classroom, office, or home. Other benefits include the ability to search the full text of a document and download images of the actual page to a computer for low-cost printing or digital cleanup to improve readability. Some examples of these resources and vendors include the following:

- *19th Century Masterfile* (Paratext) (http://www.paratext.com)
- *American Periodical Series (APS) Online* (ProQuest) ((http://www.proquest.com))
- *Ancestry Library Edition* (ProQuest) (http://www.proquest.com)
- *ARTFL* (University of Chicago) (http://humanities.uchicago.edu/orgs/ARTFL)

- *Defining Gender* (Adam Matthew Digital) (http://www.amdigital.co.uk)
- *Early American Imprints, Series 1. Evans, 1639–1800, and Series 2. Shaw-Shoemaker, 1801–1820* (Readex/Newsbank) (http://www.readex.com/readex)
- *Early English Books Online—EEBO* (ProQuest/Chadwyck-Healy) (http://www.proquest.com)
- *Eighteenth Century Collections Online—ECCO* (Gale/Cengage Learning) (http://www.gale.cengage.com)
- *Empire Online* (Adam Matthew Digital) (http://www.amdigital.co.uk)
- *Everyday Life and Women in America, c. 1820–1900* (Adam Matthew Digital) (http://www.amdigital.co.uk)
- *HarpWeek, 1857–1912* (Alexander Street Press) (http://alexanderstreet.com/index.html)
- *Making of the Modern World* (Gale/Cengage Learning) (http://www.gale.cengage.com)
- *Sabin Americana Digital Archive* (Gale/Cengage Learning) (http://www.gale.cengage.com)
- *United States Serial Set, 1817–1980* and *American State Papers* (Readex/Newsbank) (http://www.readex.com/readex)
- *U.S. Serial Set Digital Collection, 1789–1969* (formerly LexisNexis, now ProQuest) (http://www.proquest.com)
- *Women and Social Movements in the U.S.: 1600–2000* (Alexander Street Press) (http://alexanderstreet.com/index.html)

EVALUATING ELECTRONIC FULL TEXT

Historical research, no less than many other disciplines, has benefited from the information explosion. Since these materials are not inexpensive and often represent a significant commitment to a continual outlay of funds, librarians may not have complete control over whether a library picks up a subscription or not. Consortia license agreements discussed earlier can remove the librarian's influence even more. On the other hand, librarians may be asked for information and for their knowledgeable professional opinion regarding these resources as questions of subscription or cancellation arise. Therefore it is useful for librarians to be familiar with some of the resources that exist and related issues, with the understanding that both resources and issues will only increase exponentially as time goes on.

In addition to standard evaluation issues on coverage and navigation, some important questions and specific criteria history librarians should consider when evaluating electronic resources are the following:

- Can searching be limited by date range (including divisions by centuries, decades, and/or specific years)?
- How wide does the resource open up key word searching, which may be critical for alternate spellings or archaic terms?
- Does the search feature correct for or consider unusual and archaic print characters and spellings (such as an elongated *s* which looks more like an *f*, or "vvitch," instead of "witch")?

- Is the full text provided separately with or without an exact image of the page from which it is taken?

- Does it include all material, such as ads or editorials, or just featured articles?

- Are there durable links to individual pages or items?

- Is bibliographic citation information accurate and complete? (This is a serious concern with old magazines and newspapers.)

- How accurate was the OCR scanning? (Especially critical for older typefaces or badly foxed originals.)

- Was any retyping (sometimes called rekeying) done to improve search functioning?

- What is the provenance of the content?

- How complete is the resource at time of subscription? (Many primary source, full-text electronic resources are not complete, and while the resource publishers claim new material is being added on a regular basis, some companies do a better job than others.)

- What will be the demand on the resource? (One history professor and a handful of graduate students, or all students in large survey classes? Knowing this will affect the type of access and the number of simultaneous users that will need to be negotiated.)

MEDIA AND WEB-BASED MATERIALS

Video Resources

Audiovisual materials on historical subjects are often requested for classroom use. New librarians can find high-quality videos (VHS, DVD, etc.) through cable and broadcasting companies and audio-video distributors, including

- Public Broadcasting Service (PBS) (http://www.pbs.org)
- A&E (parent company of History Channel and Biography) (http://www.aetv.com)
- Discovery Channel (http://dsc.discovery.com)
- Films for the Humanities (and Sciences) (http://ffh.films.com)

The available videos from these sources will vary widely in topic, quality, and accuracy. Rather than establish standing orders for them, they should be purchased selectively based on individual requests. There may also be occasional requests for classic movies that represented the spirit of an age or cultural element. The best sources for these are online stores with a large selection of titles such as Amazon.com or Barnes and Noble.

Informative Websites

Websites require unique consideration. Many websites of interest to historians are free of charge. As such, new librarians may not feel they need to be mindful of what is freely available on the World Wide Web. However, since selection duties in many libraries also include responsibilities for identifying websites for inclusion in the catalog or maintaining subject guides and class guides, the need to pay attention to some of the Web's offerings becomes more obligatory. When dealing with contemporary history topics, especially race or ethnic histories, you will find it is critically important to scrutinize the website for provenance and applicability. In addition to the questions used to evaluate electronic full-text primary sources, here are some additional concerns history librarians will need to consider when choosing websites to add to the collection or link to from resource pages.

- Who created the site and what qualifications do they hold? The answers to these questions are not always obvious, but should be on respectable websites. There is no quality control on the Web and librarians must be wary before recommending websites.

- Is this site scholarship or propaganda? This is a particularly thorny issue as the Web provides everyone with their own "Hyde Park Speaker's Corner." Sometimes controversial claims are so outrageous they are easy to spot and avoid. Other times, the claims are more subtle and the bias is difficult to discern. Certain groups try to cloak their prejudice with an air of scholarship that is sometimes difficult for any but an expert to detect. *Caveat emptor.*

- What is the education level of the audience for whom the site was created: pre-K? Elementary? Intermediate? Secondary? Community College? Research university? Was the page created by a scholar for that scholar's students to use? Was the page created by a student? Google does not differentiate.

- When was the last update? Have any of the claims been superseded by subsequent research? Do the links still work or are most of them dead (which is very frustrating for users)?

- Does the site provide new material or just repackage existing material? Is there any added value for being on the Web? A discussion of the Dust Bowl and Great Depression era with reproductions of USDA Farm Security Administration photographs and sound recordings by popular musicians of the time such as Woody Guthrie can really bring home the despair, misery, and uncertainty of that era to modern students.

- What is the provenance of any historical documents reproduced on the website? Does the website creator own the documents? Are the scans faithful reproductions of the originals?

Here are some selected websites that are appropriate for historians, reputable, and live as of February 2012:

- Ad*Access (Duke University) (http://library.duke.edu/digitalcollections/adaccess)
- American Memory (Library of Congress) (http://memory.loc.gov/ammem/index.html)
- Center for History and New Media (George Mason University) (http://chnm.gmu.edu/index.php)
- Documenting the American South (University of North Carolina at Chapel Hill) (http://docsouth.unc.edu)
- Clio Online Fachportal für Geschischtswissenschaften (Germany) (http://www.clio-online.de/site/lang_en-US/1/Default.aspx)
- LIBRO: The Library of Iberian Resources Online (American Academy of Research Historians of Medieval Spain) (http://libro.uca.edu)
- Making of America (University of Michigan and Cornell University) (http://quod.lib.umich.edu/m/moagrp and http://cdl.library.cornell.edu/moa)
- Valley of the Shadow (University of Virginia) (http://valley.lib.virginia.edu)
- ZEIT (Das Zeit Archiv von 1946 bis 2012) (http://www.zeit.de/2012/index)

The Instruction & Research Committee of ALA's RUSA History Section has an extremely instructive website for finding and evaluating materials (especially primary sources) from the World Wide Web at http://www.ala.org/rusa/sections/history/resources/pubs/usingprimarysources.

Foreign-Language Materials

It is a requirement of almost every PhD program in history in the United States that candidates will demonstrate a reading comprehension of at least one foreign language. Two is actually more common, although some programs permit a statistical methods course to be substituted if necessary for the student's dissertation research. Historians whose area of research is outside the United States will often be fluent in the languages they need for their research. The impact of this on libraries is often numerous requests from history researchers for both primary and secondary materials in languages other than modern English. History librarians should work closely with their acquisitions departments, as purchasing and cataloging materials from foreign countries can be rather complicated and may require translation assistance from the requesting historian. Your acquisitions department may have regular vendors or suppliers for different international materials. Also, Amazon.com has branches in countries outside the United States that can facilitate finding and acquiring materials from those countries. As a result, you may get a request from a history faculty member for a book in the form of a link to the French version of Amazon. Here is just a sampling of companies and their websites that supply libraries with books from other parts of the world:

- Abebooks (Web page has links to foreign branches) (http://www.abebooks.com)
- Casalini Libri (Italy) (http://www.casalini.it)
- Otto Harrassowitz (Germany) (http://www.harrassowitz.de)
- Amazon.cn (China) (http://www.amazon.cn)
- Bagchee (India) (http://www.bagchee.com/en)
- Amazon.co.jp (Japan) (http://www.amazon.co.jp)
- Inalbooks.com (Turkey) (http://inalkitabevi.com/en)
- Books Sur (Latin America) (http://www.booksur.com)
- Sulaiman's Bookshop (Middle East) (http://sulaimansbookshop.com)

Additional information on overseas book dealers can be found on an ALA website: http://www.ala.org/CFApps/bookdealers/index.cfm.

MICROFORMS

Microform is simply an umbrella term used here for microfilm, microfiche, and microcard (sometimes called micro-opaques). Selecting microform materials can be problematic since the format is not a glamorous or popular one, even among historians who are arguably its heaviest users. It is only recently that microcards have been able to be copied, printed, or otherwise duplicated with ease by the end user. There are new products being introduced for improved scanning of all microformats, but these machines are generally in the $8,000–$10,000 range for each unit. Microforms are cumbersome materials to use with no quick access and generally require the user to be physically present in the library unless the library has implemented digital delivery on demand. However, such a service requires precise citations, and historians frequently need to browse the material thoroughly to discern which pages they need to request digitally. Large collections are expensive, generally $150 per reel, and a collection may contain dozens or even several hundred reels. Microform subscriptions to serials currently in print will need room to grow. Microform cabinets are functional with little to offer in the way of aesthetics, and large collections may require the flooring to be reinforced to handle the weight. Some microfilm materials suffer from having been poor quality at the time they were filmed; other materials have been damaged from heavy use and are all but illegible. On the other hand, because of microfilm's low-tech nature, all that is needed to read the entire contents are a light source and a magnifying lens; and basic readers are reasonably priced. Because microfilm is based on silver-halide film, it considered more archival in nature. In proper storage conditions the material will last for hundreds of years, whereas newsprint deteriorates rapidly. Though heavy, microforms still take up less space and money than purchasing the same materials in printed format. Finally, many microform collections are being scanned and then resold to libraries in a searchable, digital format at an extra cost (per the earlier discussion of electronic full-text resources).

Historians are heavy users of microform materials in their endless quest for primary sources. Many times microform is the only way certain items have been preserved, as the original no longer exists (at least on this continent). Through microforms, many libraries can offer access to rare materials that were once only the province of a few elite special collections repositories. Because of these issues, it should be up to librarians to decide, based on their institutional curricula needs and available resources, on whether to purchase microform materials or not. Regardless of whether a library decides to continue purchasing materials on microformats, because some materials coming in via interlibrary loan will be microformat, libraries must continue to support the medium with trained staff and up-to-date equipment, well maintained and in good repair. Fortunately, some reader-printers will now scan microfilm images and save the files to a USB memory device as a .pdf file. Some devices even offer autoscanning features for a reel of film. These features can breathe new life into old collections.

Librarians need to be aware that the past decade has seen a considerable amount of consolidation and mergers among microform companies. Gale Cengage (formerly Thomson Gale), for example, now owns or distributes Primary Source Media and Scholarly Resources titles in addition to their own. University Microfilms, Inc. (UMI) has been part of the ProQuest family for a number of years, which has recently merged with CSA. Both UPA and CIS were formerly part of LexisNexis, although in 2011 many of the historical congressional materials were sold off to ProQuest as LexisNexis concentrates on its legal research and current events products. Additionally, these and other companies are involved in converting portions of their collections to digital format, as discussed earlier. Companies that own the copyright to the microform version of materials are converting them to digital if they feel it would be a profitable venture. However, librarians, historians, and students need to accept that some microform collections will never be considered marketable enough to be digitized by for-profit companies, and in the current uncertain economic climate, grants for nonprofit groups to digitize materials may become quite scarce. It is for just this reason that libraries must continue to maintain and service up-to-date microform reader/printer/scanning machines in adequate numbers and be willing to purchase the format when necessary.

NEWSPAPERS

Newspapers from the time period a historian studies are invaluable primary resources. Reading a newspaper from the past is very much like stepping into a time machine. There in printed form is the information people of the time thought valuable enough to share. In one place the historian can follow discussion of local events, political debates (from local, state, and national levels), fashions of the day, even the price of bread. Often overlooked (and never indexed), advertisements can reveal a great deal of information about gender roles of the times, and even racial stereotypes. Newspapers are useful to political as well as social historians, both for their research and their teaching.

Collecting for a Balanced Viewpoint

There is a caveat that affects newspapers and to some degree magazines as well, whether in print, microform, or electronic format: the issue of bias. All news media have an editorial bias and this was even more pronounced in previous centuries than today. Horace Greeley, the outspoken antebellum reformer and abolitionist, used his newspaper, *New York Tribune*, as a platform for his antislavery agenda and opinions. Some of the major Southern newspapers in the Reconstruction era were run by members of the Ku Klux Klan, while other papers were Radical Republican sheets. The *Times* (London) has been for decades the mouthpiece of the Conservative (Tory) Party of Great Britain, and stories were reported through that political filter. Additionally, some newspapers such as the *Chicago Defender* (African American) catered to specific audiences such as ethnic minorities; other newspapers such as the numerous Yiddish- and Chinese-language newspapers published in some of America's larger cities target local populations who spoke a language other than the larger community. Newspapers are a reflection of their times, reporting important issues from the local farm report to the latest political scandal. This practice gives historians excellent opportunities to examine, compare, and contrast how certain events and ideas were viewed and acted upon by the people of the times.

The implication for libraries is that researchers will want to have more than one retrospective newspaper title available. Especially in building research collections, librarians should attempt to find newspapers published during the same times within close geographical proximity that offered different points of view. Librarians should also be aware that many cities and towns only supported a single local newspaper and the opposing editorial viewpoint may come from a nearby community. If, for example, a given town's only local newspaper openly advocated one particular political party, the librarian may find that the newspaper for the opposing party might have been published elsewhere, but was distributed on a state-wide level. Essentially, for research libraries, simply having one or two fully retrospective newspaper titles in any format at the international, national, state, and local levels will not be not sufficient for adequate teaching and research. Smaller teaching institutions can get away with fewer number and selection of titles, but should try to have at least one at the state and national level. As more companies offer retrospective newspaper titles electronically, adding these titles to the collection is becoming easier, if not less expensive, to do.

Digital Newspapers

Newspapers have also benefited from commercial digitization projects just as the collections mentioned earlier. Some notable digital newspaper collections include:

- *Dallas Morning News* (Readex/Newsbank) (http://www.readex.com/readex)
- *Early American Newspapers, 1690–1876* (Readex/Newsbank) (http://www.readex.com/readex)
- *ProQuest Historical Newspapers* (titles are purchased individually and include *New York Amsterdam News, New York Times, Wall Street Journal, Washington Post, Atlanta Constitution, Pittsburgh Courier, Los Angeles Times, Chicago Defender, Chicago Tribune, Christian Science Monitor,* et al.) (ProQuest) (http://www.proquest.com)
- *Times*-London (Gale/Cengage Learning) (http://www.gale.cengage.com)

Many of the extensive electronic collections currently available originally were available on microfilm, which may give some libraries pause before cutting huge checks to duplicate materials already on their shelves. Many libraries may already have the old University Microfilms, Inc. (UMI, now ProQuest) microfilms to major U.S. newspapers such as the *New York Times* or the *Washington Post*. Now that those newspapers and more are searchable with a considerable amount of full-text/full-image access, many librarians will have to consider carefully whether they see sufficient demand and benefits to justify the huge costs for these electronic resources and to mitigate the associated liabilities. While there are some electronic collections of primary source materials that are freely available on the Web referenced earlier in the chapter, the more extensive primary source collections are only available from commercial vendors such as ProQuest, Gale-Cengage, Readex/Newsbank, and Alexander Street Press; and unfortunately are not inexpensive. Adam Matthew Publications from the United Kingdom is still publishing collections of microforms, but they are converting materials to digital as well. For public domain materials, librarians will occasionally have a choice of platforms. Both LexisNexis (as of 2011, LexisNexis sold its congressional materials, including historical materials, to ProQuest) and Readex introduced competing versions of the U.S. Serial Set of early nineteenth-century U.S. government documents. Before deciding to commit the considerable expenditure, history librarians, preferably in conjunction with fellow librarians and perhaps even history faculty if possible, should preview, trial, and weigh carefully the benefits and liabilities associated with these collections, formats, and where applicable, Internet interfaces.

The Complete Story?

As an archival copy of newspapers, microfilm is not subject to the conditions of the *New York Times v. Tasini*, a 2001 U.S. Supreme Court case that declared the digital version constituted a separate form of publication not covered under the original copyright contract with the author. These contracts are being renegotiated, but some material in the digital versions of the *New York Times* and other newspapers is still blocked. Currently much of the blocked material is limited to maps and photographs, but library patrons need to be aware of these issues. Some search interfaces are better than others, and the displays of results or page images may be problematic.

Another important issue to consider when evaluating full-text resources and microfilm replacement is how complete the database is. Unfortunately in specific instances, a publisher (such as Readex/Newsbank) has made a conscious decision to scan some parts of existing newspaper titles, but not others, leaving a gap in coverage. Sometimes it is a matter of finding microfilm of sufficient quality to scan with little postscanning cleanup. Readex/Newsbank claims wide coverage for its *Early American Newspapers* collections. Unfortunately, the level of content actually digitized and available for use is quite shallow for many titles, in some cases having only a few issues of a title out of an entire calendar year. Although Readex/Newsbank maintains they are adding new material to the database on a constant basis, at the time of this writing it appears they are doing no more than adding more titles instead of digitizing material for titles already in the database. For historical research, this is a serious detriment. Part of what makes newspapers so useful for historical research is being able to follow the sequential manner in which a story was covered day by day or browse page by page for relevant information. In some cases, it is vital to have the ability to follow a particular event or story as it unfolds over the course of several days, weeks, months, or even years. A gap in coverage of digital collections therefore seriously and adversely affects its usefulness for historical research and should be a primary factor when evaluating digital materials. In light of the exorbitant and recurring costs associated with digital newspapers, collection decisions regarding these resources require a great deal of consideration on the part of the librarian as well as collaboration with fellow librarians and input from teaching faculty in multiple departments. Being able to appeal to a broader, interdisciplinary campus audience can help make these types of resources more attractive and purchasing a bit easier. Including faculty in the discussions also helps clearly establish expectations by faculty members ahead of time regarding the completeness of the resource, with everyone understanding that some is better than none, and they may still have to resort to using microfilm on some occasions. It also helps establish that microforms cannot be withdrawn if the electronic replacement is not fully comprehensive.

CONCLUSION

The materials that historians use come in many shapes and formats and can be found throughout the library. These materials are not limited to any specific call number range, nor should you assume historians only look at books. Because of the wide-ranging interests of historians and their students, librarians must be keenly aware that decisions affecting large sections of the collection may have an adverse impact on the teaching and research needs of students and faculty. There is often great shock and despair when a student returns to the library from spring break, only to find an important resource for his research project has been removed to a remote storage facility (true event!). This chapter has tried to examine the most common formats libraries hold and issues specific to their use by historians and students. Although the scholarly monograph is the primary form of scholarly communication for historians, information in other formats is also important for their teaching and research. Serials, microforms, e-books/e-journals, electronic databases, government materials, foreign-language materials, in addition to rare books and manuscript sources, are all important to this group of scholars. Because libraries are the main repositories for these types of resources, it is no wonder that the library is a laboratory for historians and their students.

7

SELECTION AND ACQUISITIONS TOOLS

This chapter is intended to give you some of the tools you need to continue building a collection to support historical inquiry. This is followed by a discussion of vendor services, some key selection tools, and issues to keep in mind when working with your acquisitions department. For librarians with very limited resource selection experience trying to build an understanding of basic collection development practices on the job, Peggy Johnson's book *Fundamentals of Collection Development and Management*, published by ALA, is an excellent resource to have close at hand.

Some of the issues complicating building library collections for historical teaching and research were mentioned in chapter 6. Other factors complicating the simple question of who is in charge of buying (or acquiring, or recommending) materials for history include times when people assume you work in the special collections and rare books department (even if your library doesn't have a special collections and rare books department), or that because you have given bibliographic instruction sessions to a few history classes, ergo you are also in charge of collecting materials for the history collection. Additional complications (as if we needed more) come from the complex world of budgets, book vendors, approval plans, and collection analysis. Unfortunately, it is not like contacting your local bookstore or a publisher directly and asking them to send you a dozen books. Even small academic libraries may find it easier to work through third parties (and occasionally there are economic incentives for doing so). Unless your library only adds a handful of titles to the collection each year, or has a very simple and transparent budget operation, acquiring materials is quite a complex operation.

BUDGET CONSIDERATIONS

Budget issues will affect each library differently. A community college library will have different issues than a small, private liberal arts college, even if the two colleges have similar volume count and student enrollment; and a the budget for a regional research university will look different from that of an internationally renowned, comprehensive research institution.

The degree to which history (and other subject) librarians must know or understand about an organization's budget will likewise vary by institution. Nevertheless, this section will try to give you enough basic information to allow you to be an informed consumer when budgets are discussed at organization-wide forums. In some libraries, librarians are expected to participate and offer feedback in an advisory capacity regarding vendor demonstrations, while at other libraries the opportunities for such input is quite limited.

How is the materials acquisitions budget set up at your library? This should be one of the first pieces of information new history librarians with selector responsibilities have once they assume their duties. There are numerous methods to divvy up acquisitions funds. It is not the scope of this book to judge which one may be better than the others, but rather to address them in terms of their potential impact to the history collection. While this book tries to address some of the primary methods used to divide acquisitions funds for materials, please recognize that there can be an infinite number of variations on these primary themes.

Dedicated Funds

Dedicated (or earmarked) funds are similar to your basic household budget. Generally speaking, at the beginning of each fiscal year, a specific amount of money is set in an account to be used to purchase materials. A librarian with selector responsibilities is authorized to make purchase requests for specific titles, which are purchased with money coming out of this account. At some libraries, this money might have limitations, such as prohibiting it from use for materials other than monographs. Other libraries may allow the librarian to subscribe (or renew a subscription) to a journal in the field in addition to purchasing monographs. Once the money is spent (sometimes it is *encumbered*, or held to pay for specific titles that have been requested but not invoiced), no more materials can be purchased until the next fiscal year when new money is added to the account. The acquisitions department of the library will then purchase the requested titles either directly from the publisher, or through a wholesaler. When the invoice arrives, the encumbered money is taken out of the account to pay for the titles charged to it.

Dedicated accounts are fairly easy to understand, especially if limited to materials with nonrecurring costs. You can take requests from history faculty (and even students if you want to extend the privilege) for titles they want the library to own (perhaps they want to put a title on reserve as supplementary reading for their students, or they want to consult it for their research project). Whether you spend the money in twelve months or two weeks makes no difference. You can request all the books you want until the money is gone; then you have to stop. Any requests that come in after the money is spent must wait until the next fiscal year.

Dedicated funds have some distinct advantages and disadvantages. Some librarians may appreciate a level of certainty and stability about how much can be purchased in a fiscal year. It helps in spatial planning for the amount the collection is likely to grow in a given year. Some librarians with both selector and liaison duties can use the money and ability to purchase X amount of books faculty members need and want for the collection to improve their relationship with the faculty, and thereby gain a greater understanding of what history faculty are researching and/or teaching with the direct knowledge of what titles are being requested. Conversely, sometimes the amount of money put in dedicated fund accounts is grossly insufficient to cover the teaching and/or research needs of the institution's history faculty. Some librarians (and history faculty) may see dedicated funds as being limiting or unfair, especially if the method in which decisions regarding how fund amounts are decided is not rational or transparent. Similarly, if subject specialist librarians do not have any input into how funds are distributed, it can create problems. Also, what do you do when one or two faculty members demand the library purchase all the titles on their list even though just part of one of the lists would expend all the money in the account several times over? Or, what if Dr. Jones discovers that she is being asked to teach a new course next semester and needs some extra books for the students, but the dedicated account does not have enough for more than two or three of her titles? Discretion and diplomacy must be part of the job. Having a contingency fund where possible for last-minute faculty requests can help.

Shared Accounts

Shared accounts are a bit harder to explain as there can be more variations. Essentially, instead of each selector librarian having an individual fund with which to purchase materials, there is only one large fund from which all selector librarians can draw. Without a preestablished spending limit, purchase decisions can be much more flexible. While this flexibility can foster collegiality and encourage librarians to work together to purchase needed materials (promoting librarians to look for materials usable beyond an individual faculty member or department), it can also lead to territorialism and competitive spending (a euphemism for hogging) as each tries to purchase all of her requests before anyone else. Sometimes a use-it-or-lose-it mentality sets in as everyone is trying to get their share (or what they perceive as their share) of the pie. If there are trust issues or political problems within a library, competing for shared accounts can exacerbate the issues. When moving from dedicated accounts to shared accounts, there may also be some librarians who take it as a personal affront that they were not doing their job as selector, or that some responsibility that formed a portion of their work identity is being taken away from them. A general shared account can get complicated when Dr. Smith from history comes bouncing into your office with a brochure about a really cool digital collection he saw demonstrated at his conference last week available for one-time purchase. He admits it is not cheap (several thousand dollars), but compared to some of the e-journals for chemistry, it's a bargain, right? How do you proceed? Remember what I mentioned earlier about diplomacy and discretion being important components of the job? It may take a lengthy explanation and treating for the first cup or two at the coffee house to see the larger issues at play (recurring costs vs. nonrecurring, different forms of scholarly communication among disciplines, and lack of funds caused by a down economy).

Patron-Driven Acquisitions

One of the latest trends in library acquisitions is patron-driven (also called user-driven) requests. It is a variation of shared accounts, and while it might be implemented with dedicated funds, it would require a great deal more organization and tracking than is necessary with a general pool of funds. The theory behind it seems quite rational at first: rather than questioning what titles patrons will need in the future, why not let the patrons decide what books they need and in what format? Then the library will acquire those materials. Success of this method of collection development is highly dependent upon having an efficient acquisitions department and being able to fulfill the requests in a timely manner. In some libraries, if a request for a book purchase cannot be filled within a predetermined period of time, the request may automatically roll over to the interlibrary loan (ILL) department for borrowing until a copy for purchase can be found. This is a good way to win support from library patrons and ensure that the books purchased will actually stand an excellent chance of being used.

Some library administrators see this method as a particularly attractive means of getting the most impact for money spent. The patrons get the books they want and love the library for getting the titles for them (and they will in turn support the library and promote the library to institutional administrators), the title is added to the library's collection when they are finished, library administration can show institutional administration how responsive they are being to the needs of the campus community, and little money was spent on dozens of other titles that do nothing but take up valuable real estate on library shelves. What's not to love?

Well, as the old saying goes, "The devil is in the details." As attractive as patron-driven acquisitions can be, the practice raises some especially thorny questions, particularly for academic libraries. The most important questions concern quality control and educational roles. Resolution of the questions will center on a system of checks and balances. If a library declares that any and every patron request will be honored (even if a price limit on materials is imposed), that library still runs the risk of allowing patrons to fill its shelves with popular books that have little to do with the educational mission of the library (that is, supporting the teaching and research functions of the organization of which it is part). Without being allowed to deny requests because they do not fit the collection development policy, a library may find itself spending hundreds of dollars on books about weaving and other needlework because a couple of patrons had an interest in it (despite the fact that the school has no textile arts program), or buying books of dubious academic quality on UFOs because a particular undergraduate student wanted them for a paper. During lean budget years, this could be seen as a wasteful and inappropriate use of scarce funds. Patron-driven acquisitions also question the expertise many librarians have in their subject areas. If librarians are asked to spend significant amounts of time and energy developing collection development policies that are then routinely ignored or bypassed as patron-driven requests take precedence, they will be much less likely to cheerfully promote and support future library strategic planning initiatives, seeing them as a pointless waste of their time and expertise. Patron-driven requests can too easily undermine the whole collection development planning process. Besides simply acquiring books with no planning, it seriously complicates spatial planning and data collection used to map where new shelves are needed and how the collection should be shifted to accommodate the newly purchased materials. Many undergraduates may want the library to purchase multiple copies of their textbooks and use the patron-driven request mechanism to accomplish this. How fast will such requests burn through a limited book budget without a procedure to guide the purchase of course textbooks? Only time and experience will tell.

One possible method to implement the necessary checks and balances is to require purchase requests over a specified monetary amount (or price cap) to be approved by the librarian for that area. The price cap should be logical and take into consideration the average price of materials in that field. The *Library and Book Trade Almanac* (formerly known as *The Bowker Annual*), published by Information Today, Inc., is an excellent resource to find statistical and economic data, including number of books in a field published, and average price. Very large collections or very expensive materials could go as a formal proposal to a library committee. However, defining how many unique titles in one request constitute a "large collection" cannot come from an arbitrarily determined number, but must be based on the discipline from whence it comes. The policies that govern the way the committee works must be based on the understanding of how different disciplines operate. To that end, a request for several dozen books by a history professor trying to develop a new course (or a graduate student preparing his reading list for his preliminary examinations) should not be subject to the arbitrary whims of a bureaucratic committee with little comprehension of what is expected from humanities scholarship. Any regulations imposed should ultimately serve to further the library's role of supporting the teaching and research missions of the school, not create a barrier to spending money on materials truly needed by scholars and their students. Librarians are therefore cautioned when making rules: rules, regulations, and the committees governed by them can too easily resemble a quicksand that appears stable on the surface, but quickly becomes a deadly quagmire that swallows legitimate needs for educational materials into its depths. There is also a problem in that having too many bureaucratic hoops casts the subject librarian into a negative role in the eyes of that librarian's constituents, which may ultimately undermine efforts at engagement in other areas such as library instruction or reference.

Spending Cycles

When does your library's fiscal year begin and end? When must book requests be placed in order to have the invoices paid and cleared from the ledger books before the fiscal year closes? The second question can be especially problematic. Academic libraries are heavily dependent on student labor. Acquisitions and circulation/shelving departments often have the most student workers. If a fiscal year closes early in the summer, and the school offers little in the way of summer courses, the acquisitions department may be at a loss to process requests and receive materials in a timely fashion because its student labor pool is not available. This issue may figure into setting deadlines regarding having book requests turned in, but it can also be problematic when it is out of sync with the academic calendar. For example, if a fiscal year ends in July, August, or September, and the deadline for orders is set prior to fall course schedules being posted, faculty who need the library to purchase books for course reserve materials and supplemental readings are going to be in a bind. Conversely, there are occasional windfalls late in the fiscal year that require librarians to find and turn in requests for materials on very short notice. While the latter scenario does not happen nearly enough, it often happens in the summer when many history faculty are away from campus on research trips and cannot be easily contacted for input. You may have to wing it and choose materials based on your knowledge of what courses are being taught and what research is being done. It always helps to have a variety of requests at various price-points close at hand so when your library is fortunate enough to have one of these windfalls (maybe lots more people were fined for overdue materials or a rich alumnus gave a significant donation), you can be ready to take full advantage of the situation.

Balancing between Recurring Money and One-Time Funds

The larger the organization, the more arcane and byzantine the accounting system. However, new librarians should be aware that materials funds are generally broken down into two major pots: recurring funds and one-time funds. Recurring money is dedicated to use on materials where there is a year-to-year cost. For example, serial subscriptions must be renewed each year; similarly, many database packages have annual maintenance fees. Acquisitions departments plan on these fees when drawing up the budget each year, and they generally have to add in a generous amount for inflation each year. One-time money is pretty simple: it is money used to buy specific titles and once an item is paid for and shelved, no other costs need be factored in. Granted, this is a bit oversimplified and does not take into account indirect costs of housing the book in a building with monthly electricity and custodial bills.

Serials inflation is a serious problem throughout the profession and causes no end of problems for librarians in every department. Some libraries have sacrificed their monograph budgets in order to cover the rising costs of serials. While this may appear well and good for those disciplines whose primary form of scholarly communication is the journal article, for historians and other humanities scholars, this practice is a travesty that threatens their very existence and their ability to carry out their teaching and research responsibilities. In this discipline, there must be an equitable balance between serials and monographs. Unfortunately, databases with recurring costs complicate the mix. Would the history faculty be willing to forgo requesting as many books if that money could be used for access to a primary source database such as *The Making of the Modern World* from Gale-Cengage? Is this trade-off even an option since book requests are handled through one-time funds and databases are usually recurring? Would the physics department be willing to drop a couple of journal title subscriptions to move that money over to buy more history books? Money issues can rapidly spread beyond just one department and can affect the educational role of the organization as a whole. Sometimes you, as the new history librarian, will have the opportunity for input; other times you will not. When you do, keep sight of the big picture, but remember that historians need books every bit as much as biologists need their microscopes, test tubes, and journal articles.

Paper and Binding Options

Some publishers do not print books on acid-free paper and they use paperback covers. These materials will eventually deteriorate with long-term or ongoing use. For some companies, using these print forms is a matter of cost, for they cannot afford better quality paper stock (some international publishers have this issue). Other companies simply publish for the mass market and do not take into consideration a title's potential value to future generations. In these cases, one does not have an option and can only acquire what is available. However, for a historian's long-term perspective of using the entirety of the book, the durable acid-free paper, with cloth and hard covers, should be the preferred binding. In some cases it may be more economically feasible to seek a middle ground of buying the paperback but then applying a reinforcement to the cover. Preservation-based rebinding need not be an expensive after-purchase treatment to protect the library's investment.

Good Times and Bad Times: Economic Cycles

At the time of this writing in early 2012, the U.S. economy had only just begun to recover from the shocks and recession witnessed during the first decade of the new century. Even still, there seem to be no shortage of gloom-and-doom appraisals of library economics and our trade literature has plenty of horror stories of layoffs, hiring freezes, and budget reductions. You may be in your current role as history librarian despite not having any training in the field for just this economic reason. It is sad but true that going through the exhibits at ALA and other professional conferences was a lot more fun when our budgets were flush and vendors knew we had money to spend. Others of you will snort at my previous observation and announce rhetorically, "I've worked in this library for X number of decades and we've never been able to walk though exhibits ready to spend frivolously!" We tell ourselves that the nation's economy tends to be cyclical and while it is down at the present time, it will eventually pick back up. How soon that may translate into increased acquisitions budgets for academic libraries is beyond my capacity to answer. However, we owe it to our patrons, students and faculty, to be ready for that time to come. We likewise owe it to them (and to our organization's governing bodies) to be judicious and prudent with what resources we do have at the present.

In flush times, you can be very flexible with a budget. It is easy to share when times are good. If your colleague, the librarian for the Women's Studies program, needs a couple of titles with history components, why not buy them out of your funds? Doing so is an easy way to build collegial relationships with your peers. Perhaps Dr. Jones got a bit carried away last year with his book requests; this year you can make it up to Dr. Smith, Dr. Rose, and Dr. Adams by encouraging them to get their title requests in earlier. However, in down times, when every penny spent comes under heavy scrutiny, librarians not accustomed to justifying every purchase should get used to the idea. While it may seem counter-intuitive, lean times can also encourage collaboration and cooperation with your colleagues as materials purchases may need participation from colleagues to show that a particular resource has wide appeal and would be used by more than just a handful of members of the campus community. Purchase requests may need to be piggy-backed or combined with others from fellow librarians to get more impact for the effort; and hope that the hard times will be fleeting and better times are around the corner.

BUILDING A FOUNDATION

Suppose you just learned the history department has hired three new faculty to introduce a new research area. Your library has not collected much (if any) in this area since previously there had been no need. Now, you have to support the teaching and research of new faculty in a new area. Or suppose the recently completed reaccreditation review for the college or the department was especially critical of the library for a perceived lack of support and lack of collection depth. You, as history librarian, are charged with building a foundation. How do you do that?

There are several issues at play in creating an adequate library collection to support history teaching and research. This next section will discuss some of the tools needed and suggestions for acquiring the needed resources. You will need to follow the established policies and procedures of your individual library, but some of these recommendations are good practices to use. Collection development policies need to be updated (or created if previously nonexistent) to reflect the change in direction. You will need to understand your library's acquisitions process to be able to identify quality materials, and you may even need to make recommendations to your acquisitions department on vendors and sources from which to purchase materials (especially if some of the books needed are out of print). Depending on the library's budget situation, you will probably need to negotiate some one-time, special funds to use for this endeavor. Having strong, open communication and a collaborative working environment with your acquisitions department is an important part of being an effective librarian in any discipline. Once funding has been secured, cross-checking the library's collection against a previously mentioned bibliography or a collection assessment tool (see below) and requesting titles not owned is all that remains.

Challenges of Creating a Collection Development Policy for History

The previous chapter introduced the concept of collection development policies. Now we will take a more detailed look at what one for history should contain. A collection development policy is simply a written document that describes a particular portion of a library's collection and acts as something of a road map to guide current and future selection decisions. Drawing up a collection development policy is a good exercise as it forces librarians to think seriously about both the short-term needs and long-term goals of the library's collection. However, be aware that history presents some complex challenges in making these policy statements. Because the field of history is so broad, it may be easier to make more than one policy statement (e.g., a statement for American History, a statement for Western European History, one for Latin American History, etc.). Primary source materials will almost certainly need to be treated separately. Electronic resources may require yet another policy. On the other hand, too many policies, or policies that are too complex and too rigid, will stifle and inhibit building a usable collection. Generally speaking, there are several key components that need to be in a good policy statement:

- Subject: the portion of the general collection covered by this policy.

- Purpose and scope of collection: a description of the current collection in a particular area.

- Call number classification: although extremely problematic, this is a popular method of defining specific collection. Use with caution! Perhaps investigate the possibility of expanding to "history of" sections of other call numbers.

- Collecting level: describes how comprehensive the library wishes to be in purchasing materials on this topic and subtopics.

- Nonsubject parameters: further refinement of the collecting policy based on languages, geographical coverage, formats, and level of audience.

- Related degrees and programs: additional college or university departments or programs within the curricula that might need to use these materials.

- Notes: this could contain additional information to assist librarians making collection decisions including interdisciplinary fields, intended audience, other potential users, and so forth.

- Date adopted and any revision dates.

Defining the scope of the collection should be carefully considered. While this is an opportunity to exclude certain materials and topics not studied or taught at your institution, there is the danger in being open to charges of censorship. Call numbers are a poor method of defining history and should not be the only manner of delineating which books are history books. If call numbers are used, they should be broken down into as small a division as possible (for example: LCCN HC 10–1085 Economic History or SF 41–55 Animal Culture—History). If you have questions regarding collecting levels, the Research Libraries Group (RLG) has devised an excellent conspectus which defines those levels (Johnson 2004). Keep in mind that faculty and graduate students who specialize in overseas topics will need some materials in foreign languages, not to mention that any scholars in the foreign language departments will need some materials on the histories of the countries in which their language is spoken (here is a primary example of history librarians contributing to the larger educational mission, beyond their narrow field). After being adopted, collection policies should be regularly reviewed by the current librarian for that field to ensure it matches the organization's current research and teaching needs.

There is an old admonition against being penny-wise and pound-foolish. Librarians should be aware that while collection development policy statements are useful tools to guide the selection process, these statements must never become treated as holy writ to the point where revisions cannot be made, or the policies interpreted to restrict certain opportunistic acquisitions of collections of distinction. Similarly, when the history department hires new faculty or creates a new program, the collection policy must be flexible enough to allow materials to support these new directions to be acquired with minimum interference. Conversely, librarians must be honest with themselves when drawing up these collection development statements. You may have a deep and scholarly interest in the witchcraft trials of colonial New England, but if there are no courses being taught or faculty doing research in this area, you should not set the collecting level as "Comprehensive" for books on this subject. Similarly, if you have a small history department with no faculty teaching or researching on topics about certain African states and European colonization in the nineteenth century, again there is no reason to collect at a high level. However, if you are informed that the college has hired two specialists in African Studies (one of whom is a historian), your collection policy should allow you the freedom to begin purchasing materials to support this new program. A good collection development policy looks toward the future as much as it does the present and should allow for reasonable growth.

USING APPROVAL PLANS

Approval plans are essentially contracts between the library and a third party who acts as a wholesale supplier (sometimes called a *book-jobber*) between the library and the book publishers. Librarians set parameters based on the needs of the library (generally based on the teaching and research interests of the history faculty), and the monographs budget dedicated for this use. In return, the jobber will send (with an invoice) shipments of books that it believes meet the established parameters. Depending on the agreement with the jobber, librarians may have the opportunity to review the books shipped and reject those that they feel did not meet the criteria (in a timely manner). If the jobber is also contracted to attach spine labels with call numbers and otherwise make the books shelf-ready, the ability for librarians to reject books is severely diminished.

Setting the parameters which the wholesaler will use to selectively send books is very much like creating a collection development policy. Establishing criteria for particular subjects, publishers, call numbers, prices, languages, and formats are important components for both. With most vendors, you will have the option to ask that some materials be send as *slips* or *forms*. Instead of sending the physical book, the jobber will send you a slip with a description of the title. Most of these come electronically these days, which greatly enhances the descriptive material that can be provided. Hypertext links to reviews, prizes, and other useful information can be included on the electronic slip along with typical cataloging metadata (author, title, publisher, date, call numbers, and subject headings). These forms are excellent ways to receive information about materials that may or may not be good matches for your library's collection. Sometimes you will receive a slip instead of a book because the price was too high, or the relevance of the subject matter was a little questionable, or perhaps it was a title more appropriate to a younger audience. It should be pretty obvious why a slip arrived instead of a book, but not always. You should be able to ask the vendor or your acquisitions department for an explanation. Depending on your library's particular budget situation, there may not be enough money to acquire all the desired books for the entire fiscal year. At that point, it is typical to send slips for all remaining titles. As a result, you may find it necessary to hang on to those slips until the start of the next fiscal year and then turn them in as purchase requests. Monitoring approval plans and the books and forms sent requires a significant amount of vigilance that many librarians find difficult to maintain consistently. This vigilance is not just a requirement for large research libraries. Even in lean budget years and/or at small college libraries, the plans must be closely watched to make sure only items that are really needed come in and unwanted materials are rejected in order to make the most effective use of limited funds.

Book and Serial Vendor Services

This is a time of transition because at the time of this writing (2012) two of the largest companies, Blackwell North America and YBP (affiliated with Baker & Taylor and formerly known as Yankee Book Peddler) have merged (http://www.ybp.com). Another major company in the library wholesale market is Ingram-Coutts (http://www.ingramlibrary.com). There are also companies that specialize in acquiring materials in foreign language and/or from foreign countries. Approval plans are constructed as librarians establish criteria or parameters with representatives from these companies, who then plug the parameters into a computer program. The parameters include such criteria as price, duplicate copies, types of publishers (university presses and/or select commercial houses), audience (undergraduates, graduates, et al.), monographic series, reprint editions, call number ranges, keyword topics or controlled-vocabulary subject headings, geographic scope, time periods, e-books and/or print copies, and even titles that have been awarded prizes by important professional organizations. In addition to establishing criteria to allow certain books to be sent automatically, most approval vendors can also block titles from undesirable presses (i.e., vanity presses) or reprints of old titles. Conversely, schools trying to aggressively build a collection may want reprints if they missed getting a copy when a particular title was first available.

An issue that must be accounted for in setting up approval plans for history books is the fact that a definition of what is a history book and useful to a given collection may not be obvious to whoever profiles the books for the vendor. Many are the occasions when excellent works of history fall through the cracks because the profile's definition of history was not the same as the librarian's (or a history professor's). Sometimes this happens because of a dependence on a narrow range of call numbers to define what titles are history books (Hickey and Arlen 2002; Kitchens et al. 2002). Another cause may be that the controlled vocabulary was inadequate to the task of describing a multidisciplinary work. Vigilance on the part of the librarian will catch many mistakes. Librarians should also inform faculty that no system is perfect and should a faculty member find a title that should have been delivered but was not, that faculty member should then inform the librarian, who can follow up with the vendor as to why a title was not delivered. Sometimes a minor adjustment to the profile will correct the problem, but no system is 100 percent foolproof. Use of forms as a backup review process for materials not sent can be a good tool to catch missed history items (Hickey and Arlen 2002; Kitchens et al. 2002; Metz and Foltin 1990).

Acquiring Out-of-Print Books

In history, unlike many other disciplines, especially the sciences and engineering disciplines, the definitive book on a given topic may be more than ten or even more than thirty years old. Despite this reputation, a title may not have sold adequately for a publisher to keep it in print as part of a current inventory. Alternately, as much as librarians hate to admit it, books do disappear from library shelves either through accidental damage, outright theft, or gradual deterioration and disintegration from heavy use. Either way, one may need to add a book that is not available from the normal vendors. History librarians should work closely with their acquisitions departments to search for and purchase out-of-print materials.

Two large companies specializing in out-of-print materials at this writing are Powell's, http://www.powells.com, and Alibris.com, http://www.alibris.com, who is aggressively courting library business. Establishing relationships with these companies can greatly assist finding a copy of that seminal (but esoteric) work that Distinguished Professor Smith is demanding the library find and acquire. Knowledge of or relationships with out-of-print dealers can also be useful to librarians who may be tasked with building a retrospective collection, should special funding become available to fill gaps in an existing collection. This can come up in situations where a new specialization is launched by the history department and faculty members are hired with specific funding for buying library resources in their research areas. Although rare, things like this do happen and it is always better to be prepared with some ideas to meet a variety of scenarios. Retrospective collection building is something of which all librarians, but especially history librarians, should be cognizant and at least nominally prepared because of new program directions. Familiarity with out-of-print dealers can make these endeavors much easier.

REVIEW SOURCES

Critical Scholarly Sources

Book reviews in scholarly journals of history are excellent sources of information to help new librarians make informed decisions on particular titles to purchase for the collection. Reading these critical discussions could give new history librarians an excellent overview of the book, its thesis, and its quality; all of these are important considerations that should go into selection decisions. New librarians should peruse the book reviews in the *American Historical Review* and *Reviews in American History* as well as any other journals mentioned elsewhere that are particularly applicable to a given collection. Librarians should be aware that these book reviews are often two or more years behind the book's publication, and though rare, it is not unknown for a title to be out of print before its reviews appear, requiring use of an out-of-print or used book dealer. Also, librarians should try to read more than one review of a given work before making a final decision, especially if the first review was not favorable. Poor research and writing do exist in history as in every field, but these are generally the exceptions. Philosophical differences of opinion and interpretation are more common, but it is very rare that unprofessional language is used in a review. If librarians encounter strong differences or language, they should consult a second opinion in a different journal.

There is another fine journal that should be used by many librarians, but is particularly appropriate for the history librarian: *Choice: Current Reviews for Academic Libraries*, published by the ACRL division of ALA. This journal contains hundreds of reviews of scholarly books and other media in a wide variety of topics. The reviews are often written by experts in the field for use by librarians and are frequently more timely than those published by the subject-area journals. Currently *Choice* is available in print or electronically. *Choice* reviews will be a great asset to new librarians in history in picking the best titles and building a quality collection in a cost-effective manner.

Peer Review

There are various methods librarians can use to assess the quality of books prior to purchase. The scholarly history journals have already been mentioned, but these are not the only sources for book reviews written by qualified persons. H-Net, the online community of e-mail lists for humanities scholars, has H-Review. This is a collection of book and media reviews written by subscribers from the various lists. These reviews are often posted much faster than reviews in scholarly journals and the reviewers are often faculty or graduate students in the field. Other excellent sources for quality book reviews include H. W. Wilson's *Book Review Digest* available in print or online (now as part of EBSCO), *America: History & Life*, Gale's *Book Review Index,* and ISI's citation indexes. Each source has its own criteria and different set of journals covered, but these would cover most journals accessible by librarians.

Question the Quality

It has become popular for websites such as those run by Barnes & Noble, Alibris.com, or Amazon.com to provide book reviews by customers. For many titles, especially paperback editions, these websites will include excerpts from reviews that were printed in respectable magazines or newspapers, such as those appearing in *New York Times Book Review, TLS: The Times Literary Supplement, The New York Review of Books,* or other online sources such as those published on National Public Radio's (NPR) website; thus some of the reviews appearing on these websites are of very high quality. Be aware, however, that reviews appearing on booksellers' and other Internet sites are often anonymously written by persons who may have few qualifications to write critical and meaningful reviews. A review by a disgruntled student on a book he or she had to read for a class that student did not do well in is not a review that responsible librarians should treat seriously; but if the reviewer's background is not readily apparent, all a librarian may see is a negative review. Note that a negative review is not a complete condemnation. Librarians should pay attention to why a book might have received a bad review. Perhaps the reviewer expected too much from the book, or took issue with the author's interpretation of data. If a book fits well within a collection and resources are available, you may wish to add the title, but should make this decision on a case-by-case basis. You should be very discriminating when looking for quality book reviews.

GETTING PRIZE BOOKS

Unlike some disciplines with a single premier award or small group of noteworthy prizes, there are numerous, legitimate prizes awarded by various professional history societies and learned organizations. These prizes are given for the best books, dissertations, and articles, as well as miscellaneous fellowships and research grants. Prizewinning titles are often named in the journal or newsletter of the organization that awarded the prize and its website, as well as other professional journals. Because the topics vary so widely and there are so many, it would be impossible to create a hierarchy of prizes (i.e., the prize for best book in United States history from the AHA may be different and no better or worse than a similar best book prize handed out by the OAH—Organization of American Historians). However, Columbia University awards two prizes, the Pulitzer Prize for History (awarded by the School of Journalism) and the Bancroft Prize (two awards from the University Libraries for scholarship in the fields of American history and diplomacy). These prizes are sufficiently prestigious to warrant acquisition by almost every academic library. Award-winning titles should have a high priority for history librarians, but because institutional curricula vary so greatly, it stands to reason not every library will need every award-winning title. For example, there may be little reason for a small college in the northwest to acquire a title that won the Frank L. and Harriet C. Owsley Award from the Southern Historical Association (SHA) unless there is an institutional need for a high-quality collection in southern history. Conversely, the history librarian at this same small, northwestern college will want to ensure the acquisition of a Pulitzer Prize winner or a title that won the Frederick Jackson Turner Award bestowed by the OAH as one of their top awards in United States history, as these may have a broader appeal. State and local history journals carry similar types of award announcements and librarians should not neglect acquiring these resources in addition to national- and regional-level titles. On the other hand, librarians with severely limited resources may limit their acquisitions strictly to titles that have won awards and still be able to put together a quality collection on a wide range of topics. State historical organizations award prizes for excellence and originality and librarians serving populations with interest in those areas should be aware of what is available.

Many national, state, or regional history organizations will duplicate the lists of award-winning books on their websites for any librarian to access. For example, each year the AHA awards almost two dozen book and dissertation prizes in many fields and lists previous winners on its website. A selected sample showing the range of books and prizes awarded by various organizations for the previous decade is listed here:

- AHA Herbert Baxter Adams Prize in European History (2006), *The Medici State and the Ghetto of Florence: The Construction of an Early Modern Jewish Community* by Stephanie Siegmund (Stanford University Press)

- AHA Joan Kelly Memorial Prize in Women's History (2007), *Specters of Mother India: The Global Restructuring of an Empire* by Mrinalini Sinha (Duke University Press)

- AHA Wesley-Logan Prize for books on the African Diaspora (2004), *Recreating Africa: Culture, Kinship, and Religion in the African-Portuguese World, 1441–1770* by James H. Sweet (University of North Carolina Press)

- OAH Frederick Jackson Turner prize (2005), *Impossible Subjects: Illegal Aliens and the Making of Modern America* by Mae M. Ngai (Princeton University Press)

- OAH Ray Allen Billington Prize in American Frontier History (2007), *Coyote Nation: Sexuality, Race, and Conquest in Modernizing New Mexico, 1880–1920* by Pablo R. Mitchell (University of Chicago Press)

- Texas State Historical Association (TSHA) Coral Horton Tullis Memorial Prize (2004), *The Strange Career of Bilingual Education in Texas, 1936–1981* by Carlos K. Blanton (Texas A&M University Press)

- Alabama Historical Association James F. Sulzby award for the best book on Alabama history (2001), *A Fire You Can't Put Out: The Civil Rights Life of Birmingham's Reverend Fred Shuttlesworth* by Andrew Manis (University of Alabama Press)

These are just a few examples of the numerous prizewinning books from which librarians can choose according to the needs of their collections. Note that all winning titles listed here were published by academic presses. Also notice the wide variety of topics written about: civil rights, biography, race and education, race and sexuality, religion, ethnicity, immigration, and chronologically from the medieval period to the present day. Award information can be found at each organization's Web page (remember, this is not a comprehensive list):

- The Pulitzer Prizes (http://www.pulitzer.org)
- The Bancroft Prizes (http://library.columbia.edu/eguides/amerihist/bancroft.html)
- American Historical Association (http://www.historians.org)
- Organization of American Historians (http://www.oah.org)
- Texas State Historical Association (http://www.tshaonline.org)
- Alabama Historical Association (http://www.archives.state.al.us/aha/aha.html)

Consult the websites of other professional associations and state and local history societies to find more information about what prizes they award and the criteria for those prizes (and often a list of previous winners).

ASSESSING THE COLLECTION

After a book is purchased and placed in the collection, librarians may believe their job is done, but it can be useful to be able to assess a collection's strength. This data can be used by faculty when writing grants, lobbying for new programs or additional support for existing programs, doing accreditation reviews, or by librarians looking at comparative studies with similar institutions, remote storage issues, and circulation/browse statistics. Companies that provide collection assessment tools to libraries include OCLC (http://www.oclc.org), Library Dynamics (http://librarydynamics.com), and R. R. Bowker (http://www.bowker.com). OCLC offers the WorldCat Collection Analysis Service, Library Dynamics is now the home of the North American Title Count (arguably the best-known collection assessment tool), and Bowker offers the Bowker's Book Analysis System (based on *Resources for College Libraries*, published by ACRL). Each of these systems offers the ability for librarians to gauge the strength of their collections based on detailed call number ranges (Bowker also adds the ability to use ISBNs). If your library has access to these tools, you should use them to assist in making decisions that affect the growth or shelving arrangement of the collection. However, librarians must be aware that history books can fall at any point in the LCCN range and this must be factored into results from these services. Limiting history to only LCCN C-F will miss numerous titles in social history and women's history (LCCN HN and HQ respectively), constitutional history (LCCN KF but also JK), and many more books potentially useful to historians. Any decisions affecting the collection without the understanding that history books could be anywhere may severely and adversely affect a heavy library-using group on campus.

In addition to the assessment tools just mentioned, there are other means of assessing a history collection. Bibliographies in history and numerous subfields of history abound. Because of their use by historians, bibliographies were covered in detail as part of reference materials in chapter 5. However, they do serve a valuable dual purpose as a collection development tool for the history librarian. Keeping an eye out for new, relevant bibliographies and then having a student employee verify whether the referenced books are in the collection or coming on approval is a sound strategy for history librarians. As mentioned earlier, the History Section of RUSA has produced an annual "Best Historical Materials" (formerly "Best Bibliographies in History") that is published in *RUSQ*. This list provides a librarian with an immediate starting point to the latest, quality historical materials in different areas and formats.

PROMOTING THE COLLECTIONS

With library collections, it is often tempting to take the approach exemplified by the line from an old movie, "If you build it, they will come." However, we should be cautioned, lest we more resemble the old riddle, "If a tree falls in the forest and no one is around to hear it, does it make a sound?" In other words, what good is having built a quality collection of materials (books, journals, databases, etc.), if no one on campus knows what is there to use? Promoting the collection (or more specifically, certain select items or features) to the potential audience is not a bad idea and can be accomplished in many easy ways. In tough economic times when every expenditure requires justification and administrators are looking for added value wherever it can be found, promoting and encouraging use of the collection can be a prudent step for libraries' continued funding.

One manner of promotion might include a special display in a prominent place where books written by campus faculty are displayed prior to being added to the collection. Creating such an exhibit actually promotes both the authors in addition to the library's collections. Making this promotion work will take a good bit of coordination between campus faculty, their publishers, and the library acquisitions department. On the other hand, combined with a special reception for all campus authors, such an event might be an excellent way to bring people into the library for a celebration of scholarly activity. Similarly, another promotion would be to have a prominent display or shelves dedicated to newly acquired titles. A new-book shelf where the latest titles could be browsed and even checked out a few weeks prior to going to the stacks again serves to highlight the fact that the library is bringing in fresh, new material and staying relevant to the populations it serves. Good places for a new-book shelf (or shelves) might be near the main circulation desk, or other high-traffic areas in the building. Finally, should your library be so fortunate to be able to acquire a significant title or large collection of related material: PARTY ON! Invite faculty from fields that might have an interest in the acquisition to come and celebrate. With enough advance notice, a special, scholarly colloquia could be organized around the material with experts invited from off campus to address the collection's value to their fields. Be sure to invite college and university administrators (both as a matter of course, but also to show them the value of libraries, and that your library has something very special that other schools may not have).

OPEN STACKS OR SPECIAL COLLECTIONS

Depending on the size and age of your academic institution, every now and then a patron will come to you as the history librarian with a book they found in the stacks. The patron claims it is very, very old (and it certainly looks that way) and thus, very valuable. The patron may then demand or suggest the book be locked away, placed in the special collections library, or otherwise protected from further damage or theft. Certainly tales of rare and valuable books being found on circulating stacks because no one on the library staff was aware of its value, often only after the books are recovered from thieves, are rife within our profession. Many a well-meaning patron believes he is doing us a favor by bringing these treasures to our attention before someone with fewer scruples can abscond with it or slice out the valuable illustrations. Maybe these materials are valuable, and maybe they are not. Just because a book looks ancient, with leather covers, yellowed pages, and early dates, does not mean it is actually rare and valuable (it may not even be as old as it appears). How should history librarians handle such issues?

The best manner is to accept the book from the patron with the explanation that you will do some research on it and make the best decision possible. The next step is to contact the rare book and special collections department in your library (unless you *are* the rare book/special collections librarian). Assuming you have had little training or experience in dealing with rare books, you should do what you can to make an informed opinion. Here are some steps and questions to consider:

- Look for the title on WorldCat. What other libraries have copies? Where are they housed?
- What is the condition of the copy in your hands? Are the bindings original? Has it been damaged? Are all pages present?
- Is the book heavily illustrated? Are the illustrations/maps/plates intact?
- Search for the title on some out-of-print book websites such as Powell's (www.powells.com) or Alibris (www.alibris.com). How much do they list the book for?

The book in question may not be as valuable as the patron thought. Working with your special collections librarians and relying on their expertise is generally a better way than trying to make a call such as this alone.

Another scenario that creates problems for libraries occurs when old Dr. Essex retires and wants to donate his personal book collection to the library. This is another opportunity for librarians and rare book librarians to collaborate. Rarely can entire collections simply be accepted and absorbed within a library's circulating collection. Questions to consider include:

- How many titles does the library already own?
- What condition are the books in? How many would need to be re-bound?
- Do these books fit any of the library's current collection development policies?
- Do the books support existing collections?
- How many titles would need original cataloging and are written in a foreign language?
- What are Dr. Essex's expectations regarding how many titles will be retained by the library and what will be done with the duplicates or those in no condition to circulate?
- Is Dr. Essex truly donating the books freely, or is there some expectation of remuneration or recognition for the gift?

These negotiations can become even more delicate if the donor has recently passed away and you are dealing with a bereaved spouse. In these cases, the books can often represent a sentimental value to family members who attach an inflated value to the collection. Special collections librarians, outside appraisers, and those accustomed to drawing up deeds-of-gift should be brought in, or at least consulted frequently, during these types of situations.

CONCLUSION

History librarians who also have selector responsibilities bear a heavy burden. Historians often have very high expectations of library resources to support their teaching and research and the research of their students. Given the economic crisis of the first decade of the twenty-first century, libraries that can build or maintain collections at a universally comprehensive level are a select few. Selector librarians must be much more judicious about what they purchase for the collection. Choices must reflect the current state of teaching and research topics, but must also be of sufficient quality. Additionally, librarians need to have a plan to guide future collection decisions, but with enough flexibility to change as the curricula changes. History, by virtue of its interdisciplinary nature and use of a wide variety of formats, complicates this effort. There is no one best way to build and maintain a high-quality history collection; one-size-fits-all solutions or collection criteria will invariably fail to acquire (or worse, may discard) materials certain faculty and students from the history department need. Open, two-way communication between the history faculty and the library is always encouraged, provided both sides come with open minds. Additionally, the tools mentioned in this chapter, thoughtfully used, can help you build a collection that best supports the curricula of your institution.

8

MATURING AS A
HISTORY LIBRARIAN

In keeping with its more casual tone, this final chapter reflects some of the lessons learned after being a historian and librarian for well over ten years as well as spending more than twenty-five years in higher education (either as a student or a faculty member), in a highly transitional time. When I began, college and university libraries still used card catalogs and all indexes were in print. My current laptop allows me to sit almost anywhere I have a wireless connection and conduct research on rare primary sources originally printed centuries ago. The futurists in our profession have been quick to declare the demise of print and welcome us (or drag us? or drive us?) into the information age of their brave, new, digital world. However, as Robert Darnton reminds us, the information age, which so often is used synonymously with *digital age*, is still in transition (Darnton 2011). We are only beginning to enter into a digital age, and especially in the field of history, too many resources are still in printed (or micro) formats. Therefore, we cannot completely forsake the old as we rush to embrace the new. We must have the ability and willingness to connect people with the information (in any format!) they need. Unfortunately, some of these futurists, in trying to defend their claims, have encouraged antagonistic attitudes toward printed materials that are then perpetuated by people who should know better, but do not have a suitable appreciation for Clio, her disciples, and their *modus operandi*. Some of the advice offered in this final chapter is less concerned with history in particular and could possibly be of assistance to any librarian working in higher education.

PROGRESSIVE JOURNEY

Building Relationships

Although you are working with history faculty and students as an information professional, you are also building relationships. Do not be discouraged if progress seems slow at first, because all relationships take time. Some professors will quickly jump at the opportunities you offer for library instruction and consultations, while other professors will be more standoffish. Even if faculty members are cool at first, or have the reputation of being a bit "prickly," continue to be polite. It may be these individuals just need time to warm up to others. Some professors, even if they value the library, will never vocalize their appreciation. They prefer to rely on their own skills and expect their students to get library assistance on their own. In time, they may come to value your skills and expertise, or sometimes, they never do. In this latter scenario, do not take it as a personal failure, but keep the doors open, because someday they might surprise you by contacting you for assistance. In the meantime, you will develop a number of collegial relationships with other faculty as they interact with you both for education-related needs as well as casual information inquiries.

Keeping Up Professionally

As much as possible, get involved with your state or regional and national professional associations. Keep your membership current in the American Library Association as well as your statewide library association if it offers opportunities for professional engagement with your peer group. Go to conferences whenever possible. While travel money is generally the first casualty of budget crises, look for opportunities to attend a meeting, especially if it is held in your city, or is within an easy drive (carpooling with a colleague is one way to save money). You may have to pay some of the travel or room and board out of your own pocket, but there are ways to economize when you travel. Also, explore grants and other opportunities to apply for conference funding. Many people do not bother to go to the effort because the amounts are often not sufficient to cover all expenses, but even a few hundred dollars here and there will help. It is also possible to put together packages, such as a conference registration award from New Member Round Table (NMRT) and a cash award to help with hotel or food expenses from an ACRL group. Going to meetings and exhibits can bring new inspiration for projects and services.

Attending conferences also provides a great opportunity to network with fellow librarians, which may lead to prospects for committee service or career advancement. But it is important to take the initiative to engage and reach out to others. A good example might be the RUSA History Section dinner. Even if it will not be a restaurant you would have chosen because of menu or price, in order to make connections, go ahead and sign up; and do not be afraid of introducing yourself as a new participant. It is better to be seen as a talkative novice than unapproachable. Speak up when you hear a call for volunteers for ad hoc groups, as many committees and task force groups are now doing their work virtually and have dropped or reduced the requirements for regular conference attendance.

Even if you cannot actively participate in a professional organization, stay engaged through the professional literature. Most journals provide an author's institution and e-mail for the explicit reason of allowing you to contact the authors for more information, or to let them know how much you appreciated what they wrote or how it contributed value at your institution. Reaching out to authors in this way will help you take advantage of technology in building a network of peers. Similarly, look for affordable continuing education opportunities, such as free or low-cost webinars, to get ideas on what is happening among peers or near-peers at other institutions.

Finally, it is important to look for opportunities in which you can create your own rewarding intellectual challenges within your job. Try engaging in research and publication for the profession, even if you are not at a publish-or-perish, tenure-granting institution. It will help you find connections to others that are interested in the same areas and give you insights to the publication process that will help you connect to the history faculty. You may be able to take a role in initiating a new digitization project on some unique, unpublished sources from your library's collection, or creating new finding guides or Web pages. The important factor is doing something that you personally find both intellectually stimulating and rewarding.

SETBACKS

As singer-songwriter Jimmy Buffett observed (1985), there are "good days and bad days and going half mad days." Sometimes it feels there are too many of the latter two and not enough of the first. The previous chapters talked about many issues that can make it harder or easier to be an outstanding history librarian in reaching out to users and building collections. They also discussed how you may or may not have input into or control over some institutional initiatives and organization-level decisions on priority and process. How you deal with life's daily stresses and strains will greatly affect your longevity in your position and overall professional satisfaction and engagement. Having productive outlets to get rid of stress in healthy ways is very important. These various outlets are also as diverse and unique as each person in the profession. The critical part is to take some time to recharge your internal batteries on a regular and frequent basis. Exercise is an excellent stress-buster, but it doesn't mean you have to be a gym rat. Take a walk, ride a bike. If your library has multiple floors, take the stairs instead of the elevator. If you have health problems that limit your mobility, check with your physician. Other ideas for dealing with stress could include the following:

- Attend a sporting event and cheer on your favorite team or athlete.
- Exercise your mind creatively by exploring arts programs and activities (photography, quilting, pottery, carving, etc.). Many communities offer classes for novice artists.
- Go to a concert or event (whether it is Bach or heavy metal is immaterial, as long as you like it).
- Visit a museum or gallery exhibit.
- Go outside to a park (as long as you are properly equipped for the weather conditions).
- Get together with friends for dining experiences (so long as eating or drinking to excess does not become the coping mechanism).

One final suggestion, at the risk of perpetuating a stereotype, is to curl up in your favorite chair or sofa with a good book (or e-book reader) and your favorite beverage.

Setbacks are part of life. Inevitably you will encounter frustrations or disappointments from one or more of the following:

- Colleagues let you down.
- Patrons pester you with seemingly unreasonable demands and expectations for answers to inane questions.
- Computers crash at the most inopportune moments.
- Budgets always seem to shrink rather than grow.
- Deadlines creep up on you.
- Stakes in decisions get higher and more critical.
- Simple tasks end up much more complicated than expected.

The key is that "Life happens." You can choose to withdraw (which admittedly is sometimes a good temporary solution), but beware of becoming reclusive, distant, and indifferent. However, in retreating from conflict or difficult situations, there is a danger to letting your office go from being a monastic retreat to a prison cell. Your frustration with the organization, be it library department or larger institutional issues, can get to a point where you are no longer part of the team. If not caught and checked, you can burn out. This is why having healthy outlets is so important. Having a network of colleagues who can listen sympathetically, but can also pull you out of the tendency to see a negative downward spiral, can make a huge difference. Just remember, self-righteous indignation does you no good, and grudges only injure the person who bears them. Singer-songwriter Jimmy Buffett called this one too when, in his 2006 tribute to New Orleans after Hurricane Katrina devastated the city, he realized that, at some point, we all must, "Breathe In, Breathe Out, Move On."

NAVIGATING DEPARTMENTAL POLITICS

Although it should go without saying, do not, under any circumstances, allow yourself to be drawn into departmental politics or turf wars. These squabbles can be over trivialities such as office space, choice of class schedule, or who teaches the small honors classes versus who teaches the oversized survey classes; but they can escalate to more serious issues such as who is (or is not) rewarded with an endowed chair, disciplinary focus of the department, the direction of the discipline (which can affect tenure votes), grant or fellowship support, and sabbaticals (also known as development leave time in some institutions). Although all too common in academia, these petty power games rarely accomplish anything of value to the organization as a whole, and the collateral damage of hurt feelings, damaged reputations, and desires for future revenge are rarely worth the price of victory. As the librarian for the discipline in its entirety, you must stand to serve all members equally and thus must remain above any hint of having taken sides during one of these departmental wars. You must tread very carefully during times of interdepartmental infighting. You do not want the winning side to have any reason to think you (and by extension, the library in general) supported the opposition, regardless of which side actually had the moral high ground. The best advice is to keep your eyes open, keep your mouth shut, and treat everyone fairly and openly.

Picking Your Battles

Sometimes the organizational warfare is not in the history department, but rather within the library organization itself, where you live. This necessitates some careful negotiation as you try to navigate the minefield in which you find yourself. Both higher education and libraries are going through tremendous changes, with core philosophies and practices coming under scrutiny and being challenged. A certain amount of irritation and conflict in response to change is unavoidable. Organizational strife is unpleasant; there is no easy way around it. Even being on the winning side is costly, and the toxic atmosphere of grudges and distrust may take months, if not years, to clear. There are many ways of picking your way through organizational politics, but you must recognize you cannot fight every battle. Therefore, you will need to be careful where you choose to expend your resources. Your willingness to compromise on one topic in which you are not heavily invested may earn reciprocal support for an initiative about which you do care about strongly. On the other hand, giving way on one subject that might have been easy to defend in order to keep the peace can set a dangerous precedent where adversaries will expect your acquiescence on future, related topics. Resistance at that point may be much more costly in terms of time, effort, and reputation (even if you hold the moral high ground, or believe that you do). Appeasement did not work for Europe in the late 1930s, and while the stakes within your department are nowhere near the level of World War II, standing up for what you believe is right is never wrong. However, what happens when you lose can be just as earth-shattering and can damage your psyche and professional reputation in the library. At best, the damage is short-term with opportunities to reengage on other issues in a positive way. At worst, you can misjudge the impact of your actions, end up as persona non grata, and face an uncertain future of marginalization and lack of respect from many peers.

Whether you choose to stay in your current position or begin sending out applications for jobs elsewhere should be based on more than one factor and after much soul-searching consideration. Was the issue under contention worth abandoning your position? Have you burned bridges or is the atmosphere between you and your colleagues and administrators so toxic and irreparable that leaving is the only answer? Occasionally things deteriorate so badly it does come to that. Before you commit to leaving (and you should never threaten to resign over any issue unless you are fully prepared to carry out your threat!), it is important to explore whether there is there any room for reconciliation. Nobody wants to consider these dire conditions, but rare are the organizations and relationships where there are no political squabbles. It is also important to realize that sometimes the event that led to the disenfranchisement may actually be a part of a current trend or fad in libraries, and even if you leave, you may face the same issue at your next institution. There are no perfect jobs, so explore your options carefully.

INDICATORS OF PROGRESS

Sometimes you may wonder if you are doing little more than spinning your wheels or marking time. At those moments, you will hopefully be able to reflect back, or look at a thank-you note from a class or individual, or simply experience the satisfaction of helping someone get what they need. This is why many of you do what you do. Cherish these times. Other times, however, documenting for our evaluations our progress in reaching out, teaching skills classes (and evaluating our measure of success there), building collections, and connecting people to the best resources can be difficult within highly bureaucratic structures. *Assessment* and *learning outcomes* have become buzzwords in today's accreditation processes, but it can be difficult to directly correlate time spent learning what history faculty are teaching to the number of library instruction session one is asked to conduct. In-class assessments can depend on whether a particular student has already had previous classes that introduced library services and resources. In counting quantitative statistics such as reference/consultation interactions, number of books ordered, or cataloging records produced, one risks losing sight of quality and the relationship-building that feeds to engagement by faculty and students. If possible, work to make assessment a dialogue that explores the subject knowledge expertise that is being applied to accomplish broader initiatives of history faculty developing successful research programs that support reaching tenure and promotion and teaching for undergraduate and graduate students.

SHARING KNOWLEDGE AS A SENIOR SUBJECT LIBRARIAN

Assuming that you have successfully walked political tightropes, as you stay in any position long enough, your accumulated knowledge and wisdom will come to be valued by the organization. As the recognized local expert, you will be called upon to share the skills and knowledge you have acquired through training sessions for other librarians and library staff. Often this involves either a general overview of the subject and a brief look at some of the important resources and databases, or it could also involve a more detailed examination about one resource in particular (for example, a detailed session on how to use *America: History and Life* and *Historical Abstracts*). These sessions should be looked at as opportunities to share valuable knowledge with your colleagues. Prepare for these sessions just as you would a bibliographic instruction session; this is essentially what they are. Think about what material you are being asked to cover. While your fellows are more likely to have a much better understanding about controlled-vocabulary searching and MARC records, you will need to show them how these concepts apply to historical research methods and subjects. In the same way every student will not pick up an immediate comprehension of primary sources and conducting historical research from a single 50-minute session, the same goes for staff training. You may want to develop some practice assignments typical of what they will encounter in class assignments coming to the desk as follow-up activities. Going over history resources with other subject librarians can better prepare them for the "history of . . ." discussions within their own disciplines and create a foundation for a future collaborative relationship. Additionally, once the training has been absorbed, you might have fewer interruptions from simple questions that may be answered in just a few minutes. You may be able to focus on the more difficult and challenging questions or other projects as some of the more basic questions are handled by front-line paraprofessionals and your fellow librarians. You might get enough done on other projects to take that well-deserved vacation to see the fall color in New England! Training sessions for professional/paraprofessional staff are excellent investments in your work-life balance.

CONCLUSION

As history librarians, we are entering into a new era where electronic information is becoming the norm and printed materials viewed as the less desirable format. However, as you have the opportunity, it is important to remind yourself and administrators that library science is still in a time of transition. The old ways are not yet gone, and the complete transformation to digital-only materials is far from complete, especially for a discipline that is so firmly grounded in the information of the past. Even with the rapid pace of digitization, there will still be more printed material for historians to find and use by the time I retire, though that date is still some distance away. All this is to say that we cannot completely abandon print and become bookless libraries. We must maintain and service microfilm readers. We must question the transfer process; we cannot assume digital copies are as completely useful and fully comprehensive as the printed (or microfilmed) copies and automatically discard what we have in print. For some purposes, we still need to invest in the bound codex. History students need to be taught to cast their nets far and wide, and not to fear using something just because it is made of paper.

Conversely, we need to be more involved in looking for, creating, *improving*, and acquiring digital resources. The companies who are involved in digitizing historical materials are indeed doing us good service by making these materials accessible by a much wider audience than was possible before. Students can, from their own classrooms or dorm rooms, look at some of the earliest printed books in the English language, which hopefully will inspire them and open new worlds of inquiry to them. However, as good as these digital products are, there is still much room for improvement. Key issues being encountered with current electronic resources include

- inaccurate citations;
- scanning resolution problems, particular for older handwritten manuscripts;
- gaping holes in coverage;
- OCR conversion inaccurate for indexing needs;
- inadequate search interfaces;
- search engines that return many false hits and leave some legitimate hits unfound;
- inability to view runs of sequential pages or browsing; and
- pages printed from the database that exhibit poor quality (little contrast, poor resolution, lack of bibliographic information on printout, etc.).

These issues severely limit the usefulness of these wonderful (but expensive) resources. As information specialists, we should be demanding better for our money. Also, as information specialists, we should be taking leadership roles in correcting many of these flaws.

In closing, the take-home message is that history is a very complex discipline that is extremely dependent on libraries and librarians. To the degree that everything has a history, and thus practically any topic is fair game for historical inquiry, all librarians (regardless of our specialty or job responsibilities) can be considered "Clio's helpers." From the reference librarians who help historians locate resources, to acquisitions librarians who purchase the resources (whether in print, manuscript, microform, or electronic), to cataloging librarians who assign call numbers and subject headings, all have roles to play in helping this patron group who arguably spend more time in the library than any other field, with literature and language studies being the only possible exception. Historians' ability to carry out their job responsibilities of teaching and research depend on us, and their students depend on us. It is our professional responsibility to help them.

REFERENCE LIST AND RECOMMENDED READINGS

Please note that some of these titles are now available in newer editions and/or as e-books. Websites were live as of February 2012.

American Historical Association. 2000. "'Best Practices': Encouraging Research Excellence in Postsecondary History Education." *Perspectives: Newsletter of the American Historical Association* 38 (October). Accessed February 28, 2012. http://www.historians.org/perspectives/issues/2000/0010/0010aha1.cfm.

American Library Association (ALA). Reference and User Services Association, History Section. (2003, revised 2008). "Using Primary Sources on the Web." Accessed February 28, 2012. http://www.ala.org/ala/mgrps/divs/rusa/sections/history/resources/pubs/usingprimarysources/index.cfm.

Anderson, Jill E. 2009. "Using Professional Forums to Assess Historians' E-Resource Needs." *Collection Building* 28: 4–8. doi:10.1108/01604950910928457.

Arant, Wendi, and Pixey Anne Mosley, eds. 2000. Introduction to *Library Outreach, Partnerships, and Distance Education: Reference Librarians at the Gateway*. New York: Haworth Information Press.

Arant-Kaspar, Wendi, and Candace Benefiel. 2008. "Drive-by BI: Tailored In-Class Mini-Instruction Sessions for Graduate and Upper-Level Undergraduate Courses." *Reference Services Review* 36: 39–47. doi:10.1108/00907320810852014.

Baker, Nicholson. 2001. *Double Fold: Libraries and the Assault on Paper*. New York: Random House.

Barnes, Newkirk. 2007. "Doing it All: First Year Challenges for New Academic Reference Librarians." *The Reference Librarian* 47: 51–61. doi:10.1300/J120v47n97_06.

Barnhart, F., and J. E. Pierce. 2011. "Becoming Mobile: Reference in the Ubiquitous Library." *Journal of Library Administration* 51: 279–90. doi:10.1080/01930826.2011.556942.

Barone, K. and G. B. Weathers. 2004. "Launching a Learning Community in a Small Liberal Arts University." *College & Undergraduate Libraries* 11: 1–9. doi:10.1300/J106v11n01_01.

Bee, Robert. 2008. "The Importance of Preserving Paper-Based Artifacts in a Digital Age." *Library Quarterly* 78: 179–94.

Bentley, Michael, ed. 1997. *Companion to Historiography*. London: Routledge.

Blewett, Daniel. 1995. "The Librarian Is In." *College & Research Libraries News* 10: 701–703.

Bogart, Dave, ed. 2011. *Library and Book Trade Almanac: Formerly the Bowker Annual.* 56th ed. Medford, NJ: Information Today.

Booth, Char. 2010. "Build Your Own: Instructional Literacy." *American Libraries* 41: 40–43.

Boyd, Kelly, ed. 1999. *Encyclopedia of Historians and Historical Writing.* (2 vols.) London: Fitzroy Dearborn Publishers.

Bracke, M. S., J. V. M. Hérubel, and S. M. Ward. 2010. "Some Thoughts on Opportunities for Collection Development Librarians." *Collection Management* 35: 255–59. doi:10.1080/014626 79.2010486993.

Breisach, Ernst. 2007. *Historiography: Ancient, Medieval, and Modern.* 3rd ed. Chicago: University of Chicago Press.

Bridges, Anne E. 1989. "Scholarly Book Reviews and Collection Development: A Case Study in American History." *Journal of Academic Librarianship* 15: 290–93.

Britten, W. A., and J. D. Webster. 1992. "Comparing Characteristics of Highly Circulated Titles for Demand-Driven Collection Development." *College & Research Libraries* 53: 239–48.

Buffett, Jimmy. 1985. "If the Phone Doesn't Ring, It's Me." *Last Mango in Paris.* Universal City, CA: MCA. MCA-5600. 33 1/3 rpm.

Buffett, Jimmy. 2006. "Breathe In, Breathe Out, Move On." *Take the Weather With You.* [S.l.]: RCA. RCA88697-00332-2. iTunes.

Carignan, Yvonne, Danielle DuMerer, Susan Klier Koutsky, Eric N. Lindquist, Kara M. Mc-Clurken, and Douglas P. McElrath. 2005. *Who Wants Yesterday's Papers? Essays on the Value of Printed Materials in the Digital Age.* Lanham: Scarecrow Press.

Case, Donald O. 1991. "The Collection and Use of Information by Some American Historians: A Study of Motives and Methodology." *Library Quarterly* 61: 61–82.

Cox, Richard J. 2002. *Vandals in the Stacks? A Response to Nicholson Baker's Assault on Libraries.* Westport: Greenwood Press.

Crotts, Joe. 1999. "Subject Usage and Funding of Library Monographs." *College & Research Libraries* 60: 261–73.

Dalton, Margaret S., and Laurie Charnigo. 2004. "Historians and Their Information Sources." *College & Research Libraries* 65: 400–425.

D'Aniello, Charles A., ed. 1993. *Teaching Bibliographic Skills in History: A Sourcebook for Historians and Librarians.* Westport: Greenwood Press.

Darnton, Robert. 2009. *The Case for Books: Past, Present, and Future.* New York: Public Affairs.

Darton, Robert. 2011. "5 Myths About the 'Information Age.'" *Chronicle of Higher Education.* April 17.

Delgadillo, R. and B. P. Lynch. 1999. "Future Historians: Their Quest for Information." *College & Research Libraries* 60: 245–59.

East, John W. 2010. "'The Rolls Royce of the Library Reference Collection': The Subject Encyclopedia in the Age of Wikipedia." *Reference & User Services Quarterly* 50: 162–69.

Fabian, C. A., C. D'Aniello, C. Tysick, and M. Morin. 2003. "Multiple Models for Library Outreach Initiatives." *The Reference Librarian* 39: 39–55. doi:10.1300/J120v39n82_04.

Foner, Eric., ed. 1997. *The New American History.* Rev. ed. Philadelphia: Temple University Press.

Fritze, Ronald H., Brian E. Coutts, and Louis A. Vyhnanek. 2004. *Reference Sources in History: An Introductory Guide.* 2nd ed. Santa Barbara: ABC-Clio.

Galgano, M. J., J. C. Arndt, and R. M. Hyser. 2008. *Doing History: Research and Writing in the Digital Age.* Boston: Thomson-Wadsworth.

Gilman, Todd. 2009. "Not Enough Time in the Library: Just Because Your Students are Computer-Literate Doesn't Mean They are Research-Literate." *The Chronicle of Higher Education.* May 14.

Gilmore, M. B., and D. O. Case. 1992. "Historians, Books, Computers, and the Library." *Library Trends* 40: 667–86.

Gracy, David B. II. 2001. "'Just as I have Written It': A Study of the Authenticity of the Manuscript of José Enrique de la Peña's Account of the Texas Campaign." *Southwestern Historical Quarterly* 105: 254–91.

Grafton, Anthony. 2007. "Future Reading: Digitization and Its Discontents." *The New Yorker.* November 5. Accessed August 17, 2011. http://www.newyorker.com.

Grassian, Esther S., and Joan R. Kaplowitz. 2009. *Information Literacy Instruction: Theory and Practice.* 2nd ed. New York: Neal-Schuman.

Groneman, William, and James E. Crisp. 1995. "The Account of José Enrique de la Peña." *Military History of the West* 25: 129–65.

Hamaker, Charles A. 1992. "Management Data for Selection Decisions in Building Library Collections." *Journal of Library Administration* 17: 71–97.

Hamaker, Charles A. 1995. "Time Series Circulation Data for Collection Development or: You Can't Intuit That." *Library Acquisitions: Practice & Theory* 19: 191–95.

Hartley, L. P. 1954. *The Go-Between.* New York: Knopf.

Hartman, D. K. and C. A. D'Aniello. 2006. "Subscribe to an Online Directory Today, Frustrate a Researcher Tomorrow." *College & Research Libraries News* 67: 222–26.

Hickey, D., and S. Arlen. 2002. "Falling Through the Cracks: Just How Much 'History' is History?" *Library Collections, Acquisitions, & Technical Services* 26: 97–106.

Howard, Jennifer. 2008. "New Ratings of Humanities Journals Do More than Rank—They Rankle." *The Chronicle of Higher Education.* October 10.

Howard, Jennifer. 2009. "Humanities Journals Confront Identity Crisis." *The Chronicle of Higher Education.* March 27.

Hunt, Lynn, ed. 1989. *The New Cultural History.* Berkeley: University of California Press.

Iggers, Georg G. 1993. "Historical Methodologies and Research." In *Teaching Bibliographic Skills in History: A Sourcebook for Historians and Librarians*, edited by Charles A. D'Aniello. Westport, CT: Greenwood Press.

Intner, S. S., and E. Futas. 1996. "The Role and Impact of Library of Congress Classification on the Assessment of Women's Studies Collections." *Library Acquisitions: Practice and Theory* 20: 267–79.

Jacobs, Warren N. 2010. "Embedded Librarianship Is a Winning Proposition." *Education Libraries* 33: 3–10.

Johnson, C. M., S. K. McCord, and S. Walter. 2003. "Instructional Outreach Across the Curriculum: Enhancing the Liaison Role at a Research University." *The Reference Librarian* 39: 19–37. doi:10.1300/J120v39n82_03.

Johnson, Peggy. 2004. *Fundamentals of Collection Development & Management.* Chicago: American Library Association.

Katz, William A. 2002. *Introduction to Reference Work.* 2 vols. 8th ed. Boston: McGraw-Hill.

King, Jack B. 1994. "History Research into the 21st Century." *The Reference Librarian* 47: 89–108.

Kitchens, Joel D. 2001. "Practical Help for the History B.I.: Making Your One-Shot Count." *Research Strategies* 18: 63–73.

Kitchens, Joel D., Pixey Anne Mosley, Jon C. Marner, and Anne L. Highsmith. 2002. "Defining History for Library Statistics, or Everything Has a History." *Journal of Academic Librarianship* 28: 211–23.

Kuchi, T., L. B. Mullen, and S. Tama-Bartels. 2004. "Librarians without Borders: Reaching Out to Students at a Campus Center." *Reference & User Services Quarterly* 43: 310–17.

LaGuardia, Cheryl. 2011. "Library Instruction in the Digital Age." *Journal of Library Administration* 51: 301–308. doi:10.1080/01930826.2011.556948.

Manning, Patrick. 2004. "Gutenberg-e: Electronic Entry to the Historical Professoriate." *American Historical Review*. 109: 1505–26. doi:10.1086/530934.

McGrath, W. E., D. J. Simon, and E. Bullard. 1979. "Ethnocentricity and Cross-Disciplinary Circulation." *College & Research Libraries* 40: 511–18.

Meier, John J. 2010. "Solutions for the New Subject Specialist Librarian." *Endnotes* 1: F1–F10.

Metz, P., and B. Foltin, Jr. 1990. "'A Social History of Madness'—or Who's Buying this Round? Anticipating and Avoiding Gaps in Collection Development." *College & Research Libraries* 51: 33–39.

Mosley, Pixey Anne. 1998. "Creating a Library Assignment Workshop for University Faculty." *Journal of Academic Librarianship* 24: 33–41.

Natowitz, A., and P. W. Carlo. 1997. "Evaluating Review Content for Book Selection: An Analysis of American History Reviews in *Choice, American Historical Review*, and *Journal of American History*." *College & Research Libraries* 58: 322–35.

Novick, Peter. 1988. *That Noble Dream: The "Objectivity Question" and the American Historical Profession*. Cambridge: Cambridge University Press.

Nunn, B., and E. Ruane. 2011. "Marketing Gets Personal: Promoting Reference Staff to Reach Users." *Journal of Library Administration* 51: 291–300. doi:10.1080/01930826.2011.556945.

Oshinsky, David. 2000. "The Humpty Dumpty of Scholarship." *New York Times*. August 26.

Perez, Alice J., ed. 2004. *Reference Collection Development: A Manual*. 2nd ed. Chicago: American Library Association.

Presnell, Jenny L. 2007. *The Information-Literate Historian: A Guide to Research for History Students*. New York: Oxford University Press.

Reynolds, Leslie J., Carmelita Pickett, Wyoma vanDuinkerken, Jane Smith, Jeanne Harrell, and Sandra Tucker. 2010. "User-Driven Acquisitions: Allowing Patron Requests to Drive Collection Development in an Academic Library." *Collection Management* 35: 244–54. doi:10.1080/01462679.2010.486992.

Ritter, Harry. 1993. "History and Interdisciplinary History." In *Teaching Bibliographic Skills in History: A Sourcebook for Historians and Librarians*, edited by Charles A. D'Aniello. Westport, CT: Greenwood Press.

Robin, Ron. 2004. *Scandals and Scoundrels: Seven Cases that Shook the Academy*. Berkeley: University of California Press.

Rosenzweig, Roy. 2011. *Clio Wired: The Future of the Past in the Digital Age*. New York: Columbia University Press.

Singer, Carol A. 2010. "Ready Reference Collections: A History." *Reference & User Services Quarterly* 49: 253–64.

Sowards, Steven W. 1988. "Historical Fabrications in Library Collections." *Collection Management* 10: 81–88.

Stambaugh, Emily. 2011. Storage interest/discussion group. Library Leadership and Management Association (LLAMA) discussion/interest group meeting at the January, 2011 Mid-Winter Meeting of the American Library Association in San Diego, CA.

Stieg, Margaret F. 1986. *The Origin and Development of Scholarly Historical Periodicals*. Tuscaloosa: University of Alabama Press.

Stieg, Margaret F. 1990. "Technology and the Concept of Reference, or What Will Happen to the Milkman's Cow?" *Library Journal* 115: 45–49.

Tucker, J. C., J. Bullian, and M. C. Torrence. 2003. "Collaborate or Die! Collection Development in Today's Academic Library." *The Reference Librarian* 40: 219–36. doi:10.1300J120v40n83_18.

Van Dyk, Gerrit. 2011. "Interlibrary Loan Purchase-On-Demand: A Misleading Literature." *Library Collections, Acquisitions, & Technical Services* 35:83–89. doi:10.1016/j.lcats.2011.04.001.

Wilson, M. C., and H. Edleman. 1996. "Collection Development in an Interdisciplinary Context." *Journal of Academic Librarianship* 22: 195–200.

Winks, Robin W., ed. 1969. *The Historian as Detective: Essays on Evidence.* New York: Harper Torchbooks.

Wissoker, Ken. 2000. "Negotiating a Passage between Disciplinary Borders." *Chronicle of Higher Education.* April 14.

Yale University Library. 2008. "Primary Sources at Yale." Accessed February 28, 2012.. http://www.yale.edu/collections_collaborative/primarysources/primarysources.html.

INDEX

Accreditation reports, 32–33
ACRL. *See under* American Library
    Association
American Historical Association, 8, 19,
    74–75
American Historical Review, 8, 16, 76
American Library Association: Reference
    and User Services Association, 18–22;
    Association of College and Research
    Libraries, 18–19, 22
American West, 4, 16
Annales school, 15
Approval plans, 95–96
Archives, 46–47
Articles, scholarly, 7, 11
Assignments. *See* Course assignments
Atlantic World, 3, 8
Audiovisual resources, 79
Awards, 98–100
Axtell, James, 16

Beard, Charles and Mary, 16
Bellesiles, Michael A., 73–74
Bibliographic instruction.
    See Library instruction
Bibliographies, 38–39
Bolton, Herbert, 4, 6
Book reviews, 6, 97–98
Borderlands, 16
Braudel, Fernand, 15
Building a new collection, 93
Building faculty relationships, 24–28, 50–51,
    65–68, 105–6, 108–9

Call numbers, 9, 12, 69–70, 100
Calloway, Colin, 16
Candidate tours, 32
Cataloging practices, 42–43
Charleston Conference, 20
Class guides. *See* Web guides
Collection depth, 28, 35–36, 47–49, 94–95, 100
Collection development policies, 69–85,
    93–95
Community colleges, 28–29, 30
Comparative borders, 3–4, 8
Continuing education, 17
    See also Professional development
Course assignments, 31–32, 37–40,
    56–62, 64–67

Dates, in search terms, 42–43
Davis, Natalie Zemon, 15, 43
Degler, Carl, 16
Diasporas, 8
Digital reproductions, 5, 12–13
Dunning, William A., 16

E-books, 7, 70–71
Embedded librarianship, 50–51

Febvre, Lucien, 15
Foner, Eric, 16, 17
Foucault, Michel, 5, 15
Franklin, John Hope, 16
Freedom of Information Act, 13–14
"Frontier thesis," 16
Funding for collections, 88–89, 91–93

Gaddis, John Lewis, 16
Genealogy, 18, 33–34
Gifts, 102
Google searching, 40
Government documents, 5, 11–12, 13–14,
　　33, 45–46
Gramsci, Antonio, 15

H-HistBibl. *See* H-Net
Historical misrepresentation, 40–41, 72–73
Historical research: availability of materials,
　　13–15, 35–36; definition and scope, 1–2,
　　3–4; methodologies, 2–3, 4–5, 7, 12–13;
　　overlap with other areas, 8–10, 60–61;
　　specializations, 3–4, 7–8, 30–31; text-
　　books, 74
Historiography, 1, 3, 15–16, 59
History conferences, 20–22
H-Net, 7, 20, 98
Hoaxes. *See* Holocaust denial; Historical
　　misrepresentation
Hobsbaum, Eric, 15
Hofstadter, Richard, 16
Holocaust denial, 40–41, 73

Indexes 37–39, 44–45, 63
Information literacy, 24–25, 27, 31–32,
　　40–41, 55–56
Interlibrary services, 6, 13, 14, 26–27, 28, 70

Journals, 74–77
JSTOR, 8, 26, 75–76

Lamar, Howard, 16
LCSH. *See* Subject headings
LeFeber, Walter, 16
Liberal arts colleges, 28–29, 30
Library instruction, 62–65, 67–69
Limerick, Patricia Nelson, 16
Local community needs, 33–34
LOEX conference, 20

Magazines, 5, 11–12. *See also* Journals
Manuscripts, 5, 11–12
Marketing, 25–26, 50–51, 101
Mentors, 17–18, 110
Microforms, 5–6, 11–13, 81–82
Miller, Perry, 15
Monographs: collecting, 70–71; published
　　by historians, 6; used for research, 4, 5,
　　11–12, 29–30
Myths, 2, 13–14, 15–16, 33–34

Newspapers 5, 11–12, 61–62, 83–85
New York Times v. Tasini, 84–85

Office hours, 50
Optical Character Recognition (OCR), 6
Out of print, 96–97
Outreach, 23–28, 50–51, 65–68,
　　105–106

Patron driven acquisition, 89–91
Phi Alpha Theta, 60
Political survival skills, 108–9
Primary sources, 2, 4, 5–6, 29, 31,
　　44–46, 63–64, 82; electronic full
　　text 77–79
Privacy, 41–42, 46
Professional development, 17–22, 106–7
Project MUSE, 8
Promotion and
　　tenure support, 29–30

Reference interview, 36–40
Resources: availability 13–14, 35–36,
　　96–97; full text 77–79, 83–85;
　　identifying faculty needs 26–33;
　　reference sources 43–45, 47–49.
　　See also Websites
Royal Historical Society, 21

Said, Edward, 15
Scanning, 5–6, 12–13
Scholarly publishers, 71–72
Search terms, 14–15, 41–43, 62
Secondary sources, 4, 5–6, 31
Serials inflation, 92
Social history, 2–3, 7–8, 15–16
Southern Historical Association, 21
Subject headings, 43

Talking to faculty, 17, 24–28
Teaching support, 30–32
Textbooks, 74
Thompson, E. P., 4–5, 15
Turner, Frederick Jackson, 4, 16

Ulrich, Laurel Thatcher, 15–16
University press, 71–72

Virtual reference, 37–39, 41–42
Von Ranke, Leopold, 1–2, 15

Weber, David J., 16
Web guides, 51–52
Websites, 79–81
Weems, Parson, 15
Western Historical Association, 21
Woodward, C. Vann, 4, 16
Work-life balance, 107–8